K'etetaalkkaanee
The One Who Paddled Among the People and Animals

K'etetaalkkaanee
The One Who Paddled Among the People and Animals

The Story of an Ancient Traveler
told by Catherine Attla
transcribed and translated by Eliza Jones
illustrated by Cindy Davis

Yukon Koyukuk School District
and
Alaska Native Language Center
1990

Printed in the United States of America

Library of Congress Cataloging-in-Publication Data
Attla, Catherine
K'etetaalkkaanee, the one who paddled among the people and animals: the story of an ancient traveler / told by Catherine Attla ; transcribed and translated by Eliza Jones ; illustrated by Cindy Davis
p. cm.
English and Koyukon Athabaskan on facing columns
ISBN 1-55500-038-X
1. Koyukon Indians--Legends. 2. Koyukon language--Texts. I. Jones, Eliza. II. Title. III. Title: The one who paddled among the people and animals
E99.K79A875 1990 90-12731
398.2'089972-dc20 CIP

First printing 1990 1,300 copies
Second printing 2001 300 copies
Third printing 2017 75 copies
Address correspondence to
Alaska Native Language Center
University of Alaska Fairbanks
P.O. Box 757680
Fairbanks, Ak 99775-7680

Contents

Foreword vi
Introduction viii
Acknowledgments xiii
The Episodes
Saanlaaghedoh: Fish Camp 1
Zʉhge: Camp Robber 5
Ggʉh: Rabbit 11
K'ets'eghʉltoon Denaa Yoo: The Chickadee People 15
Tsonggude, Eł Ahone, Delbegge:
Willow Grouse, Spruce Grouse, and Ptarmigan 19
Tenh Noo K'etełkkʉyenh:
The One Who Spears Through the Ice 23
Belaazone: Otter 27
Tseyaa Nʉgh Neso: Grandpa, I Have Come to You 33
Negoodzeghe: Horned Owl 37
Sooge: Marten 41
Nełtseeł: Wolverine 49
Behookkaay Denaa: Shovel Man 55
K'etleedzode: Hawk Owl 59
Delo' Ghʉ Nołedoyee:
The One Married to His Own Hand 67
Neełkk'aa Oyht'aan:
The One with Snowshoes Bent up on Both Ends 71
Ts'eyee Gheeyo Denh: Where He Spent the Spring 75
Gełtl: Fishhook 89
Begho Kk'ʉsk'eghedeeghuł'o' Soo' Gho Kk'ʉsk'eghedee'onh:
How Unlikely to be Hanging By the Neck From That 95
Taahgoodze Tl'en Ghʉ K'enaaneełtl'eł Denh:
When He Shot an Arrow Into Mink's Leg 103
Dotson' Deghuskk'oze Etlyeł Denh:
When He Grabbed Raven's Beak 111
Boogh Tleełtl'en Bʉgh Neeghodenaaneeyo Denh:
Where His Older Brother's Skull Came Ashore to Him 119
Sołt'aanh Betl'ots'eyegheełtaanh Ghenee Nesoogheetleyh:
He Made a Grave for the Girl Who Had Been Given to Him 127
Boogh Tson' Gheneede Ghʉ Neekkaanh Denh:
When He Came to His Enslaved Older Brother 133
K'oyeedenaa Yoo: Little People 139
Yełkuh Sołt'aanh: Giant Woman 147

Foreword

Students of the oral literatures of the world are extremely fortunate to have presented here a rich version of the classic Koyukon tale, *K'etetaalkkaanee*. Perhaps the longest of the Koyukon traditional narratives (*kk'edonts'ednee*), it recounts the epic journey of a traveler, strong in spirit power, who traverses the North. As K'etetaalkkaanee follows his destined path, he effects the transformation of animals, establishes customs, defines features of the physical world, and illustrates practical wisdom. Many of the Northern native peoples have stories of an ancient traveler who, on his journey, meets amazing beings and helps transform the world. Though K'etetaalkkaanee often acts like culture heroes, monster slayers, transformers and tricksters in other Native American oral traditions, he always transcends such categories. He may trick a creature or transform beings into animals, slay a cannibal or teach a lesson in cultural values, but these are by-products of the mysterious spiritual quest at the heart of his story. This quest leads him from home in search of the medicine power of which he has dreamed.

Through these episodes, the audience is guided through Story Time long ago, when people and animals could talk to each other. More importantly though, the audience is constantly reminded that the search for spirit power and its exercise change the world now as they did long ago. The world K'etetaalkkaanee influenced can be seen today and is still in dynamic equilibrium.

The movement of most traditional Native American narratives is from a world of all possibility to one with fixed and clearly defined natures and forms. As the stories develop, human and animal cultural values are formed, social customs are established, and species personalities are defined. In *K'etetaalkkaanee* the world takes form before the eyes of our imagination.

K'etetaalkkaanee has a special relationship with the animals of interior Alaska. He visits their homes and, during his sleep, they are transformed. He hunts them but also acts as their prey. He describes and defines characteristics that we can still see in animals today, and at the end of the story he even becomes one. Throughout, we are reminded of how similar the animal and human realms really are, and how deserving of understanding and respect both are.

The story of K'etetaalkkaanee functions on many levels at once. Most immediately, audiences will respond to a dramatic character who journeys from one surprising and suspenseful episode to the next. However, Attla is quick to point out the cultural values also expressed in these episodes. Moreover, while the story delineates many tenets of cultural wisdom, it also delineates social mores and the practical wisdom of survival in the North. Also at the foundation of these cultural functions is the sense that this story and other *kk'edonts'ednee* are prayers for short winters and good lives, that those who tell the old stories, who know them and live with them, will be blessed with long, lucky lives. Remembering these things might help the reader who is uncertain of the sense of action and motivation in the story to gain some perspective. In the face of a story that has satisfied generations of listeners and found a central place in a rich body of oral literature, the only thing "primitive" is our criticism and understanding.

Catherine Attla is a consummate storyteller, ideally suited to present Koyukon stories in a rich, evocative context. Her knowledge of *kk'edonts'ednee* is extensive and detailed. Her storytelling keeps her audiences, both Koyukon and non-Koyukon, firmly in mind as she skillfully weaves narratives that satisfy both while retaining the precise perceptions of the old storytelling language and techniques. Jones' hand in the transcription and translation is always sure and informative. She captures the rich texture of the original language and performance in her translations. In this volume as well as the two preceding ones, the superb collaboration of Attla and Jones allows Koyukon *kk'edonts'ednee* to take its place in the first ranks of world oral literatures.

James Ruppert
University of Alaska Fairbanks

Introduction

K'etetaalkkaanee, the epic tale of a traveler who paddled all summer and walked all winter, is Catherine Attla's third volume of stories in the Koyukon genre called *kk'edonts'ednee*. *K'etetaalkkaanee*, like the two previous volumes — *Sitsiy Yʉgh Noholnik Ts'in': As My Grandfather Told It* and *Bakk'aatʉgh Ts'ʉhʉniy: Stories We Live By* — takes place in the mythical past, in Story Time long ago, when people and animals could talk with one another.

The episodes of *K'etetaalkkaanee* form what folklorists call a cycle, a group of stories united by one character. The *K'etetaalkkaanee* cycle differs from the Raven cycle in Koyukon tradition in that it must be told in its entirety and in a specific order. Catherine Attla has made it clear that in the *K'etetaalkkaanee* cycle, unity and sequence of the episodes are vital. If the story is told during the time for storytelling, between early winter and mid-winter, at least a week is needed, with several episodes being recounted each evening. As long as *K'etetaalkkaanee* is being told, no other story should be started.

This story cycle is about a boy who grows up, leaves his mother's home and goes on a long journey to live out his dreams and gain medicine power. From the beginning, readers and listeners know that K'etetaalkkaanee will leave home and that he will meet adventures and obstacles. The central question is whether he will overcome these obstacles and come back to his mother. If he does, he will be the first in his family to return from a spritual medicine journey.

This is a common theme in Native American literature. With each dangerous encounter, K'etetaalkkaanee's medicine or spiritual power increases. The more difficult and dangerous the encounter, the more power he gains. His two brothers, who began similar journeys before him, did not have enough power to overcome certain obstacles. K'etetaalkkaanee discovers that one was killed and the other enslaved. Koyukon stories usually end as the hero either returns home a powerful medicine man or meets an obstacle that he cannot overcome.

Storytelling is an oral art among the Athabaskan people, and merely writing down the words cannot convey the story's entire meaning. Although the stories were traditionally told in the dark, many non-verbal clues accompanied them. The telling of the stories was, and is, considered as important as the content. Part of the enjoyment derived from a story comes from the way it is told. In this respect, the Athabaskan storytelling tradition is similar to the non-Athabaskan genre of drama.

Storytellers are not allowed to make changes or additions when telling *kk'edonts'ednee*, but they often make side comments and discuss the events in a story. They might also make adjustments for a particular audience, leaving out, for example, some things that might be inappropriate for children. Catherine Attla made several asides while telling *K'etetaalkkaanee*. At one point, when K'etetaalkkaanee remarked on the weakness of the soup that the camp robber family gave him, she said, "Why didn't he just keep quiet? He had to be fussy even though he did not carry his own food." In another episode, when K'etetaalkkaanee became afraid of the power of the medicine man in mink's village, Catherine Attla said, "It serves him right that he was afraid." Until that point, K'etetaalkkaanee had been smug about his own power. Humility is an important virtue in Athabaskan culture.

Catherine Attla learned the story of K'etetaalkkaanee from her late grandfather Francis Olin, a medicine man of the Koyukuk River. She said, however, that her grandfather never told her the end of the story. Out of curiosity, she finally asked her grandmother, who told her the ending once, and she remembered it from that one telling. Catherine Attla often speaks of her belief in the religious importance of these stories. She believes that they have been filling the spiritual need of people for years, and they have been the Bible of the Athabaskan people. To many of the Koyukon people who are Christian, the stories are like another testament, and telling them is like praying. Traditional stories are meant to entertain, educate and inspire — to cause the reader or listener to think. People believe that telling these stories not only instructs and entertains, but also shortens the winter and brings good fortune to the storyteller as well as the audience.

K'etetaalkkaanee was recorded by Catherine Attla in *Denaakk'e* (the Koyukon Athabaskan language), transcribed and translated by Eliza

Jones, and edited by Chad Thompson and Eliza Jones. We have tried to make our translations as true to the original *Denaakk'e* as possible. In balancing literary style and linguistic accuracy, we have used these guidelines: If the *Denaakk'e* sounds smooth but the English translation sounds awkward, the translation is a poor one. However, if, in an attempt to improve the translation's literary quality, so many liberties have been taken that the original meaning is lost, the translation is also poor.

We have followed the policies of translation outlined in the introduction to *Bakk'aatugh Ts'uhuniy*. Those policies are as follows:

Pronouns. We often used a full noun where the *Denaakk'e* has only a pronoun. For example, what in *Denaakk'e* is "He walked up to him" we translate as "K'etetaalkkaanee walked up to him."

The word *K'etetaalkkaanee* appears only a few times in *Denaakk'e* but is used throughout the English text. K'etetaalkkaanee's true name, Betohoh, is mentioned only twice — once by the narrator in the first episode, "Fish Camp," and once by the woman in "Camp Robber."

First person plural pronouns. While narrating *kk'edonts'ednee*, storytellers often use the first person plural *we* to refer to characters at the forefront of the action. In this book we translated these forms as *he*, *the man*, or *K'etetaalkkaanee.* Most often they are assigned to the main character of the story. Catherine Attla uses it for the Marten Man, Wolverine, and the man in the story "How Unlikely to be Hanging by the Neck From That." In the Mink story she uses the first person plural pronoun to refer to K'etetaalkkaanee.

The first person plural pronoun is also used to refer to an unspecified individual and is translated as *someone.* In the Marten story, for example, when Catherine says that someone is following K'etetaalkkaanee, she literally says, "we are following him."

Tone of voice. While telling stories, Catherine Attla used various voices to convey meaning and characterization. Where these conveyances are important, we added an adverb to indicate the intended mood.

Sentences. For stylistic reasons, we sometimes translated two or more *Denaakk'e* sentences as one English sentence or one *Denaakk'e* sentence as two or more English sentences.

Connectors. The *Denaakk'e* words *dehoon, ts'uh* and *ło'ts'eyuh* can be given English meanings, but sometimes we had to rely on context and style to determine how to translate them. For example, we translated the word *ts'ʉh* in various places as "so," "then," or "and."

Exclamations. We have assigned translations to *Denaakk'e* exclamations even though they might at times sound colloquial. The word *doo'* is the only one we left untranslated. It can be either an exclamation of mild surprise or a validation of one's expectations, similar to the English "Well, what do you know?"

Emphasis. When telling these stories, Catherine Attla emphasized certain words by drawing them out or saying them louder than others. We indicate drawn out words with three hyphens after a vowel (*Hʉdee—yh!*), and loud words with capital letters (Raven said, "*GGAAKK!*").

Ellipsis. In the *Denaakk'e* version, words or phrases are occasionally omitted. Such omissions are readily understood by *Denaakk'e* speakers, but because they might confuse English speakers, we included the missing words or phrases in the translations. We used ellipsis (...) in the *Denaakk'e* version.

Terms of address. Throughout the story, people address K'etetaalkkaanee in kinship terms even though they are not actually related to him. Traditional Athabaskan people refer to one another as uncle, nephew, grandparents or grandchildren, depending on age differences. Similarly, the term *ggenaa'*, "friend," or *seggenaa'*, "my friend," is used to refer to anyone the same age and sex as the speaker, even though that person might be a stranger. We translated kinship terms literally even though they are not taken as such.

Politeness. In at least two situations, Koyukon people traditionally use the third person singular (he/she) when talking to one person, and the third person plural (they) when talking to two or more people. Those situations are 1) out of politeness and respect and 2) in confrontations or reprimands. In the Camp Robber story, Mrs. Camp Robber uses the third person form out of respect, probably because she is a woman and because K'etetaalkkaanee is powerful. In the Wolverine story, Wolverine addresses K'etetaalkkaanee in the third person when he challenges him to fix his tooth.

Indirect reference or circumlocution. Athabaskans avoid direct reference to certain things or activities that involve spiritual power, luck or skill, especially things associated with medicine power or hunting. For example, in the story "The One With Snowshoes Bent up on Both Ends," when K'etetaalkkaanee comes to a bear in its den, the word *bear* is not mentioned because the bear is too powerful to be named directly.

Format. These translations are phrase-for-phrase rather than word-for-word. Each *Denaakk'e* paragraph in a left-hand column has a corresponding English translation in the right-hand column. The lines in some cases do not match exactly because a *Denaakk'e* phrase might take two lines and the English translation only one, or vice versa.

The Koyukon orthography has been changed since the first two volumes of the Catherine Attla texts were published. The *i* and single *a* are now written as *e*, and the *tł* is now written as *tl*.

While for clarity we have taken liberties with the meanings of some words or phrases, we feel that the intended overall meaning is intact.

Eliza Jones
Chad Thompson
Alaska Native Language Center

Acknowledgments

We especially want to thank Cindy Davis for bringing these stories to life with her illustrations. Tom Alton and Lorraine Elder are to be thanked for editing, typesetting and preparing this book for publication. Chad Thompson typed the original translation from Eliza Jones' tape recorded translation. We also thank Joe Kwaraceius for help with final proofreading.

Saanlaaghedoh
Fish Camp

Go hełde koon K'etetaalkkaanee beezneeyee. Hʉydok'egheeyo ts'e saan k'egheekkaanh. Kk'ʉdaa tl'ogho eey denaak'ekk'edonts'ednee' dodeenaalee heyʉghʉ noholnegee.

Yegge gheel ts'ʉhʉt'aanh degheel yoogh saanlaaghedoh k'edaadletl'ee. Ło'ts'eyʉh hʉtlenh ghʉ nelneyh. Degheel yegge Betohoh beezneeyee go keel letaanh, beł neltenh, beł neltenh. Yoogh kk'onheedeneeyh de heghetekk'e neełlot ts'e beł neltenh. Ts'ʉh yoogh go hʉtlenh ghʉ nelneyh aatloogh tobaan yenk'eedet'oł hu gheel kk'o'eedoyh. Huyeł zʉhge ło'ts'eyʉh k'ekk'oon ghʉ yʉh tełneeyh. Go k'ekk'oon yełzooy seełtonolyaayh ts'en'. K'ekk'oon k'eełekk'ee nelaanh ts'en' go noolaagh kk'oone'.

Ts'ʉh noyeetent'oyh, noyeetent'oyh. Ts'ʉh gheel yoodetaatlleeyh, le'on aahaa. Huyeł k'eełekk'ee dzoten kk'e k'edaaneełnenh t'aanh. Ts'ʉh

This is a story called K'etetaalkkaanee[1] It is about a man who walked all winter and paddled all summer. It is the longest of the stories that the people used to tell.

In the time very long ago, many people were staying at a fish camp. People were working very hard, putting away fish. There was a boy named Betohoh who slept and slept and slept. Between the short periods of time that he worked, he seemed to sleep a lot. One day he was walking around on the beach where people were cutting fish. Some camp robbers were busy carrying away fish eggs.[2] They were taking the fish eggs and carrying them away one egg at a time.

They kept carrying the eggs away, bit by bit. Then Betohoh began to throw rocks at them. He hit one of them on the leg and broke it. The camp robber flew off

1. K'etetaalkkaanee means "The One Who Paddled among the People and Animals."

2. The camp robber is a bird also known as the gray jay, Canada jay or whiskey jack.

yoogh bedzode kk'e k'edaalnenh ts'e bedzode nedebeł dehoon gheel no'eet'ʉkk.

with its leg dangling limply in the air.

Ts'ʉh yoogh eet kk'ʉdaa saan hʉgheelet. Hʉyts'edogho ode letaanh. Neełlot ts'e k'etetaayh.

The summer passed. The boy slept the entire fall. He always slept late.

Yooghedone hełde ʉhts'e heghe'ene yegge denaa hʉn neeł-lotts'e beł eetenleteeyh. Yoogh ts'aak'eedaah dehoon yegge denaa gheel beł neltenh. Et'eeyło ts'aa-hootee'oyenh ts'ednee.

It is said that long ago, if a young person slept late like that, if he or she kept sleeping after everyone else had risen, it was a sign that the young person was to become a medicine person.[3]

Ʉhts'e dent'aa. Deyełneyoo kkaa kk'e huyeen' ts'aa'elek.

That was what was happening to Betohoh. He would get up after everyone else in the family had gotten up.

Dehoon gheel boogh kkaa gheel haahedeedeyhtl.K'eełekk'ee heelaanh ts'e haahedee'ʉs, haahe-dee'ʉs ts'ʉh naahełdeyhdlaa. Kk'ʉdaa hʉn koon ʉdenh yaan' yoogh gheel sołt'aanh hebeyeł hoolaanh eehu hee. Kk'ʉdaa hʉn koon ʉdenh yeen' donh yeł ledo.

Before this, his brothers had all left home. They had left one by one and had never returned. He was the only one remaining—he might have had a sister too, but we don't know. At that time, he was the only one who remained with his mother.

Hʉyeł hʉn kk'ʉdaa yoogh hʉyh hoolaanh. Ts'ʉh nohoołekk'otl. Hʉyeł gheel hʉn, "Eenaa, haadee-taaghsoł."

Then it was winter. It was after it had become cold. He said, "Mom, I'm leaving."

3. Traditionally, young people were trained to rise early in the morning. It would have been unusual for a young person to sleep late except if he or she were becoming a medicine person.

"Tlegede donodetaałenee' gonee? Nedaadenh go hʉts'e dʉht'aanh? Ees noogh kkaa k'eełekk'enh zokk'ʉł no'eełdoyaa haadeegheedeyhdlee kkaa. Go ło nedaats'e dʉht'aa ts'e go dedʉhnee? Nenh zokk'ʉł seyeł leedo," yedetaalnee' eehoo.

"What is he talking about? Where is everybody going? Your brothers have all left and not one has returned. What is wrong with all of you, anyway? You, at least, should stay with me," she begged him, futilely.

Eenh hoghaadleneek, ts'ʉh, "Eenaa, ts'aal haadeetaaghesoł," nee. Doo' baanh doyedeneegheełk'eet eehoo dehoon haadeeyo.

He got ready and said, "It will be okay, Mom. I'm going to leave anyway." His mother tried to persuade him to stay, but to no avail; he left.

Zʉhge
Camp Robber

De yoogh nedaats'e neek'o-hoł. Huyeł hʉn do'o hʉn naakk-lookkʉno hołeghee'o de hʉn hʉtaatl-'aanh. Eet hʉts'e taalyo. Eet neeneeyo, ts'ʉh doogh dekkaa' dełgheł.

He had been walking for a long time when he caught sight of an underground house from which smoke was rising. He started to walk toward it. He went up to it and brushed his feet.

Go haahaa helodelnenh ts'en'. Go hełde ts'eedaahaa kk'oyenee-'eedeleede daa' hełde yʉh hedaa-heto'ʉstl. Go hełde yoogh don hełde ʉhdehot'eek ts'ednee. No'o dzo-ghoteey łaałdoy neehee'os ts'ʉh hedekkaa' hedełgheł.

This is how they used to knock: If somebody had bad intentions, he would not knock—he would walk right in. It is said that that is what they used to do long ago. When they came to the entryway they brushed their feet.

Ts'ʉh hedoneeyo. Huyeł go hʉn sołt'aanh saakkaay yeł yeh ledo.

He went inside. A woman and her children were in the house.

Huyeł hʉn aanee hʉn hek'edaa-neełkooł. Ts'ede etlkooł. At'eeyło bet'oh ts'etltaanee.

Something by the back wall was covered with a blanket. A blanket was lying there. Apparently a sick person lay under it.

Huyeł hʉn go sołt'aanh hʉn, "Anaa sekoye, nedaats'e koon ghe-hol det'aanh? Kk'ʉdaa betsey nen' nee'eeltl'et denh. Kk'ʉdaa betsey denaataatldlee' denh," nee.

The woman said, "My dear grandchild, where did he come from? His grandfather is bedridden back there. His grandfather is about to cause us to starve." [1]

1. The woman used the third person singular forms "he" and "his" instead of directly addressing him with "you" and "your." Also, she called him "grandchild" even though they were not related. In *Denaakk'e* (Koyukon) it is common to address someone as a grandchild if

Dehoon nonł baabe yoho ekk'o-hootaatl-'onh.

Huyeł gheel, "Eey, huts'e zo soo' deggeldo ts'e det'aan! Yegge saan kk'oontlee' k'ek'edeenaadlekoot de k'edzoten k'oodeleeyh ghu detaał-t'aanee. Nugh ees Betohoh Tsee-k'aal dzoten kk'e k'edaaneełnenh. Ts'uh nonee ees uhts'e haahaa kk'udaa nen' nee'eeltl'et," beeznee.

Yoogh kk'oon' denk'ee gheel hun hedononaat'onh ts'uh nonł eeydee gheel etlbaats. Toleł etl-tseenh. Ts'uhu kk'udaa nonł go, "Neeyonenh, donł kk'udaa k'ee-honh," beeznee. "Neeyonenh," hedegheenee' ts'uhuyaan'. Ts'uh kk'udaa nonł baabe ghu neeneeyo. Kk'udaa gheel k'etlekk'aat gheel-hee. Ts'uh k'etaalhon'. Ts'uh toleł dedeedekkonh, go kk'oon' toleł. Ts'uh yedenoonh, ts'e yedenoonh. Huyeł kk'oon' gheel hudegaał belo toneghee'onee, ts'e go dodnee nek'uh? K'edodlekel dehoonh. "Dzo! Selo tok'enghee'onh," nee. Ts'uh kk'aatugh hełde koon doogh ode uhts'e dehednee.

Quickly, she began to cook some food in the center of the house.

"Is that the only reason Betohoh awoke? Last summer he threw rocks at the leg of the one who was putting away fish eggs. It was then that Betohoh broke his grandfather's leg with a rock. That is why he is bedridden now," she told him.

She brought in about four fish eggs and boiled them. She made a broth from them. She said, "Newcomer, come eat." They used to call any newcomer *neeyonenh.*[2] He went to the place where the food was being served. He must have been hungry. He began to eat. He put the fish egg broth up to his mouth. He drank it and drank it. Finally one fish egg floated into his mouth. Why didn't he just keep quiet? He had to be fussy even though he did not carry his own food. He said, "Finally! One little fish egg floated into my mouth." People still say these words the way they are said in this story.[3]

---

he or she is young enough to be someone's grandchild. Similarly, if people are old enough to be grandparents, they are often referred to that way. When the woman said that the grandfather was about to cause the family to starve, she meant that he was unable to hunt to bring them food.

2. *Neeyonenh* means "the one who came."

3. If people swallow something solid while drinking thin or watery soup, they say, *"Dzo selo tok'enghee'onh,"* "finally, a pellet floated into my mouth."

Doogh kk'ʉdaa betsoo yek'egheełon'. "Koyh, go nedaats'e hʉyeł zee neghooł'aan'," yełnee.

After his grandmother had fed him, she said, "Grandchild, could you possibly look at his leg and use whatever power you might have."

Go hełde soo' yʉgh neetoneyhtl yoodnee ts'ʉh. Go deyenenh nelaanh ts'e gheel heyeneeł'aanee. Nedaats'e ghulaa'.

She said this thinking that K'etetaalkkaanee might be able to help him. She must have noticed something about him that indicated that he was a medicine person. I don't know.

Huyeł hʉn kk'ʉdaa k'egheehon' de hʉtl'oghʉnh nonee yʉgh neeneeyo. Ts'ʉh, "Nedaadenh?" yełnee. Doogh dedzoten yogees gheel bezo neeneetonh. Go hʉn koon k'etsaan' beltl'oonh. At'eeyło k'etsaan' bezaatltl'oonh go beltoolneh ts'ʉh. Ts'ʉh doogh eeydee gheel baats'edeneetonh. Ts'ʉh yedełdooł gheelhee. Huyeł hʉn neełghʉ noyedaaneełdokk.

After he ate, K'etetaalkkaanee went back to the sick person and asked him, "Where does it hurt?" Then the camp robber exposed his poor old, skinny leg. A blade of grass had been used as a splint. Apparently they had tied grass to his leg after it broke. K'etetaalkkaanee took off the blade of grass and blew repeatedly on the leg, making sputtering noises.[4] He healed it.

"Anaa sekoye, dodenaahoodegheeł'aan koon betsey yendenaa'eetaatldlee' denh." Go k'ughulaagh edenh nee ts'en'.

"My dear grandchild, how fortunate that he came to us just as his grandfather was about to cause us to starve." She meant that there would have been no one to catch game for them.

Kk'ʉdaa henaaldzet. Yʉh sots'eeyh aahaa t'aanh dehenaah.

Then they all went to bed. They were so happy.

---

4. Koyukon medicine people used to blow on wounds to help them heal.

Yoogh nedaats'e neeholeł kk'odehun', ło go hʉn ts'aano'eedelet. "Haa! Łoghʉn hot'aanh denh," yeneelenh. "Łoghʉn k'edenhne yeł tlede esleet," yeneelenh. Ts'ʉh doogh degge daaneełneek. Hʉyeł hʉn haadok'edeełneeyaa. Ts'ʉh kk'ʉdaa doogh hʉneeł'aanh. Go t'aanh yʉh k'etlkoot go heyogho k'egheehonee.

At some time during the morning he woke up. He thought, "Oh, yes, I remember. I'm spending the night with some strangers." He got up. Everything was quiet. He looked around. He looked around for food leftover from supper.

Go hełde neteehde hʉyaan' k'odon' yooghedone kk'edonts'ednee koonh. Neteehde hʉyaan' k'ehehonh dehoon dzaan hʉgheelek. Hełts'en' hegho k'ehon kkaa ts'aahedeh. Ts'ʉh hełts'en' koon k'enonodeneyh ts'ʉhʉyaan' hoogheelaa' hednee.

It is said that long ago people ate only two meals a day; this was true for our more recent ancestors and for people of story time. They ate only twice a day. They ate in the evening and they ate when they got up in the morning. In fact, they say that people used to cook only one big meal a day.[5]

Ʉhts'e gheel dehoot'aa hee donł t'aanh k'etlkoot doogh eeydee ghʉ degge daaneełneek. Doogh hʉn tl'oyee zʉhge tson yaan' hoolaanh. Ts'e hogho doogh yeh hʉneeł'aanh. Hʉyeł doogh hʉn koon k'ekkelaa. Ts'ʉh yoogh go k'edolkeł gheelhee nedaats'e ghulaa'? Tleeno'eedeyo huyeł do'oogh hʉn ts'ebaa kkaakenh te zʉhge henodelnaah. At'eeyło k'enhetllaat. Kk'ʉdaa yeetlkkonh ts'ʉh haanodeedeyo.

That is why he looked for leftovers after he got up. All he could find were some camp robber droppings in the dish. He looked all around the house. Nobody was around. Maybe he was carrying some food with him. Maybe he did not even eat. He went back outside, and there were many camp robbers among the bases of the spruce trees. Apparently the people had become camp robbers. After it became daylight, he left.

5. They would eat the leftovers for breakfast the following morning.

Ggʉh
Rabbit

Ts'ʉh koon kk'ʉdaa haanodeedeyo. Ts'ʉh doogh ghehoł, ghehoł, ghehoł. Kk'ʉdaa yoogh koon nedaats'e neenok'eedeyo. Hʉyeł hʉn yoogh nohʉtaałdonh denh gheel hʉgh taalyo. Go nohʉtaałdonh denh hʉgh ghehoł. Hʉyeł doogh hʉn ggʉh nonotlee'eeltonh. Ts'ʉh go de'oy ghʉ dek'ol haadeneelo. Dek'ol dekk'e yeghee'ʉgh yeł dołok'eghaaltonh. Ts'ʉh go daangge kk'ʉdaa eet daa'en ghehoł. Hʉyeł do'o hʉn yeh hoolaanh. Eet gheel go ede det'aanh ts'e łaałdoy neeneeyo. Ts'ʉh dekkaa' dełgheł. Ts'ʉh kk'ʉdaa naayegge hedoneeyo.

He left once again. He walked and walked and walked. Once again, he walked for a long time. He came upon a place where there was a strip of land between two lakes. While taking a shortcut across it, he came upon a rabbit trail. He removed the foot straps from his snowshoes and set a spring-pole snare. Then he resumed walking. He came upon a house. As was his custom, he went to the entryway, brushed his feet, and went inside.

Huyeł go hʉn koon sołt'aanh dedenaa' kkaa yeł yeh ledo. O bekkun' gheel koon ledohee nedaats'e ghulaa'? Ts'ʉh kk'ʉdaa heyek'etaatłłon'. Huyeł hʉn yʉhʉ baabe kk'e de'eet'eyee baabe eedleneyaayee eenh go baabe nelaanh gheel heyegheełon'. Ts'ʉhʉ et'eeyło koon dekenh.

A woman and her children were inside the house. I don't know whether her husband was there or not. They started to feed him. It did not taste like food to him when he ate it, but he ate it anyway. Apparently it was sticks.

At'eeyło yoogh ggʉh yehonee k'olgees delogh yoogh ts'etl deloghevee gheel go ehonee hʉyh te.

Rabbits eat them. They eat only willow shoots and willow tips in the winter.

Ts'ʉh kk'ʉdaa go yenk'eheehon'

They ate and sat around. Then

ts'e hedaadletl'ee. Hʉyeɬ yegge keel hʉn bedenaa' keel k'eeɬekk'enh degge daaneeɬneegenh hʉn notaaɬetl'oon'. Ggʉh leɬ ggoɬtlaakk nenodolkooɬ, ggʉh leɬ kkaakenh koonh ggʉh leɬ ts'eh koonh, ggʉh leɬ gets koonh. Yʉh ggʉh leɬ yaan' yee eɬetl'oonh. Naa'en t'aanh tleetaalyo. Ts'e yoogh dehoot'aa. Huyeɬ hʉn hedono'eeɬdoyaa. Tledaaɬ. Hedono'eeɬdoyaa eenhde huyeɬ gheel henaaldzedee. Hʉyeɬ go keel tleetaalyoy baanh gheel hʉn k'edetaaldlee'.

one of the woman's sons got up and began to get dressed. He put on a rabbit-skin parka, as well as rabbit-skin boots, a rabbit-skin hat, and rabbit-skin mittens. Everything he wore was made from rabbit skin. Then he went outside. He was gone a long time. He never returned home. It became dark. He still had not come home when they went to bed. The mother of the boy who had left began to sing.

"Kk'odone done seyoze yoze kk'oonootseeyh okko tleetaaleyo. Adenh tlede hʉgheelet. Nogheeldoyhtl, nogheeldoyhtl. Kk'odone done seyoze yoze kk'oonootseeyh okko tleetaaleyo. Adenh tlede hʉgheelet. Nogheeldoyhtl, nogheeldoyhtl."

"Early yesterday, my little son went out for sandbar willows. The night passed without him. Be coming home, be coming home. Early yesterday, my little son went out for sandbar willows. The night passed without him. Be coming home, be coming home."

Tlaa hedodetoneyhdlenh tlede dodetaatlneek. Go kk'oonootseeyh gheel go nooyoogh kk'ʉyloo nodenolyaalee tledone, eeydee ent'aa go kk'oonootseeyh yeɬneeyee. Kk'ʉdaa yʉh haahaa beɬ eetenooldaah ts'e hedeenh. Gheel, "Hudee---yh! Hʉ endenk'e beɬ eetenolten ɬo donts'e denaadeyoghee?" nee.

When would she ever stop? She sang through the entire night. *Kk'oonootseeyh* are the small willows that grow on sandbars. He was not able to get any sleep because of her singing. Finally he said, "Hey! When is that one singing over there going to stop?"

Huyeɬ hedodegheetset, go soɬt'aanh. Naa'en hʉts'e ɬaaɬdoyegge daa'en hʉts'e hʉdetaaɬeggut. Tleentl'ok'edodetluɬ eetl'ekk.

Suddenly, the woman stopped. He heard thumping noises going out the door. In the dark he heard some things hopping out the door.

Degheel kk'ʉdaa yʉh beł ee-naadledaakk. Go yʉh beł ede nee-dozaaneełtaanh ts'ʉh hobełye-gheełtaanh. Ts'e yoogh nedaats'e neeholeł huyeł hʉn ts'aano'eedelet.

"Haa! Łoghʉne hot'aanh denh," yeneelenh. Kk'ʉdaa koon degge daaneełneek. Ts'ʉh doogh hʉneeł'aanh. Hʉyeł doogh hʉnde yeh k'ekkelaa. Ts'e hogho doogh hʉneeł'aanh.

Hʉyeł doogh hʉn et'eeyło ggʉh doodze laaghe doogh hʉn ggʉh doodze yaan' hoolaanh. Kk'ʉdaa doo' donługh hʉn koon kk'oonoo-tseeyh yaan' tl'oyee hoolaanh go k'egheelkoot hu. Ts'ʉh dekenh yaan' gheehon' ts'e ło go k'etle-kk'aa dent'aa. Yenodetoolney edenh.

Ts'ʉh gheel, "Haa ho do'o nohʉtaałdonh det'aanh sek'ol yeł dołok'eghaalstonh," yeneelenh. "Tlaa eey zee eeydee no'eenaaghe-ge'aan'," yeneelenh. Ts'ʉh naa'en eeydee ts'e notaałeyo. Do'o zo ggʉh nogheek'et. At'eeyło eeydee go bekk'aa tlede k'ets'egheetseghee. At'eeyło ełeluyh yegge kk'odon done tleetaalyo done. Ts'ʉh kk'ʉdaa eeydee no'eeltaanh. Ts'ʉh kk'ʉdaa eeydee enodaadleneek. Ggʉh naaghedon'. Ts'ʉh kk'ʉdaa eeydee kkaa koon haanodeedeyo.

Finally, he went to sleep. Because he had not been able to sleep before that, he went right to sleep. I don't know how long he slept before he woke up.

He thought, "Oh! Yes, I remember." He got up and looked around. Nobody was there. He looked around in the kitchen area.

All that was left were some rabbit droppings. He also found some plates with willows on them where the leftover food from supper had been. That was why he had not felt full the night before, even though he had eaten a full meal. He had nothing to cook.

Then he thought, "Oh, yes, I set a spring-pole snare yesterday with my snowshoe straps." He thought, "Maybe I'll go check it, even though I may not have caught anything." He went to check it. A rabbit was hanging in the snare. It was the one that someone had cried for all night. Apparently it had been snared early in the day, soon after it had gone out. He took the rabbit to the house and cooked it. He ate the rabbit and started walking again.

K'ets'eghʉltoon Denaa Yoo
The Chickadee People

Ts'ʉh kk'ʉdaa yooghe koon ghehoł, ghehoł. Ahuyeł kk'ʉdaa yoogh nedaats'e neek'ohoł. Ts'ʉh kk'ʉdaa yoogh ghehoł, ghehoł. Go ʉhdon kk'obełyeetltaanh hu gheel go gheholee. Ts'ʉh yoogh yʉh deten noghedoł kk'aant'aa gheelhee. Kk'ʉdaa yooghe ghehoł. Hʉyeł yegge hʉn koon hołeghee'o. Eet hʉts'e taalyo. Kk'ʉdaa yoogh eet neeyo. Go ede det'aanh ts'e łaałdoy neeneeyo. Ts'ʉh dekkaa' dełgheł. Ts'ʉh hedotaalyo. Go hʉnde koon yeh ts'eledzok. Dedenaa' kkaa lon, denaa yoze kkaa gheel yeh daadletl'ee. Hededenaa' kkaa yeł yeh heldo, neełkkun' kkaa.

"Hee! Denaa edenh de debaa koon det'aanh. Hʉts'e dogheet'aa' koon det'aanh?" hednee gheelhee.

Ts'ʉh kk'ʉdaa, "Heen', nʉgh hedonok'eneelkoot nʉgh ts'enee'ots," nee gheel go denaa.

Naa'en t'aanh tleetaadletluh, go sołt'aanh. Yooghe ode dehoot'aa. Huyeł hʉn do'ots'e hʉn notluhtl loy yoogh k'eggootl he'etlt'eh. At'eeyło kk'ʉdaa hedonok'etaadlekoot.

He continued to walk and walk. He had been walking for a long time. He walked and walked. He was walking where he had already journeyed in his sleep. It was as if he were backtracking. He was walking along. Way off in the distance he could see a trail of smoke extending upward. He began to walk toward it. He walked up to it. As usual, he went up to the entryway, brushed his feet, and went inside. Many people were in the house. A big family of small people was living there. A man and his wife and their children lived there.

"Hey! There are no people around here. Where did he come from?" they said happily.

The man said, "Honey, bring in some food. We have a visitor."

The woman rushed out. She was gone for a while. She came back with a scraper that had on its edge some scrapings from a skin. Apparently those scrapings were the food she was bringing in to cook.

Go hełde uhts'e hukk'aatugh ees hełde koon yegge huyts'en' te yoogh beleł daałetl'edze ehelaayh tuh eeydee leł en daadeyus ts'e daahedełkeyhtl. Go Grandpa gheelaa' ees sunughul uhdaaghet'aan'. Eeydee hełde yuh huyee ts'aadełkeyhtl go k'ets'eghultoon. At'eeyło yooghe uh det'aanh gheelhee eeydee gheel needaalkoodee.

This is why, in the fall when people catch the thing with the black skin, they hang up the skin with the inside turned outward.[1] I saw my grandpa do that. The chickadees clean it up well, and store it as their food supply.

"Hudee---yh! Ło'ts'e sedzoghe dehoot'aa de gen egholgudzeyee do'ots'e deył'aanee?" koon ts'eyeneelenh gheelhee.

Then he thought to himself, "Oh my! I'm really hungry. Is that all she's going to cook?"

Soot'e yuh kk'e ts'enaal'onh gheelhee ts'e go, go sołt'aanh gheel, "Yee! Hebeghudaa' neeyo, k'edeeteey denosloh," nee. Go k'edeeteey nekoghe enotaaletlneek, nee ts'en'.

The woman must have seen the expression on his face, and said while she was preparing the food, "Oh dear! Their cousin came, and I overdid it." She was saying that there would be plenty of food.

Ts'uh nee, ts'e gheel kk'udaa nonłe yeyeł dok'edaal'onh. Huyeł gheel hun koon nekoh ts'e dedeyoh, go k'eggootl baadze'. My! Hun koon yuh k'enaałdon'. Kk'udaa yoogh hełts'edogho hooneelet. Ts'uh gheel kk'udaa henaaldzet. Naaltaanh.

Saying that, she put a pot with the scrapings in it over the fire. Soon the boiled scrapings expanded. My! When he ate, he had more than enough. The evening passed. They all went to bed. He went to bed.

Yooghe tlede hugheelet łonh.

The night passed. As usual, he

1. "The thing with the black skin" refers to a black bear. The word "bear" was seldom spoken by traditional Koyukon people. When people caught a bear, they hung the skin away from where people were staying, usually near the den where the bear had been killed. When they hung it up, they turned the fleshy side outward so that the chickadees could pick at it.

Dehoon go ede det'aanh ts'e ts'aano'eedelet. Ts'ʉh, "O łoghʉne!" yeneelenh. Kk'ʉdaa koon degge daaneełneek. Huyeł haadok'edeełeneeyaa, go ede dehoot'aa' ts'en'. Donłughe hʉneeł'aanh. Dooghe hʉn saanhggaagge tson kk'aant'aay yaan' gheel tl'oyee hoolaanh go t'aanh k'egheełkoot denh.

Ts'ʉh daa'en tleeneeyo. Huyeł do'ooghe hʉn koon k'ets'eghʉltoon yʉh ts'ebaa kkaakenh te henodelnaah. Ʉhts'e hʉkk'aatʉgh ees koon det'aanh. At'eeyło hʉyh hʉggaagge laaghe.

Go yet o yooghe gen gheel naaghodonoo? Ts'ʉh kk'ʉdaa yooghe koon haanodeedeyo.

woke up and thought "Oh, yes!" He got up. As usual, the house was still. He looked around. All that was left in the house were bird droppings in the dish where the food had been.

He went outside. He saw many chickadees around the base of a spruce tree. To this day it is like that. There are always a lot of winter birds around the bases of the spruce trees.

He must have eaten something and then left.

Tsonggude, Eł Ahone, Delbegge

Willow Grouse, Spruce Grouse, And Ptarmigan

Ts'ʉh ghehoł, ghehoł, ghehoł. Yoogh gheel tlede nenaa'elet. Kk'ʉdaa yooghe koon nedaats'e neek'ohoł.

Hen ghehoł hen hʉkk'aatʉgh ghehoł. Huyeł nedaa yoodo hʉn koon yʉh tenkk'e denaa aahaa dohʉnaah. Kk'ʉdaa eet hʉts'e ghehoł. At'eeyło koon tenkk'e bekkaa'eekkoy det'aanh. Tl'ogho yʉh denaa aahaa yʉh nedaats'e ghulaa' dehoot'aa gheelhee go denaa lonh ts'en'. Kk'ʉdaa eet neeneeyo. Ts'ʉh doogh denaa kk'aabaaghe lehaanh gheelhee.

Huyeł yegge denaa hʉn, "Ggenaa, go ło neenyohee?" yełnee.

"Oho', go ees et'egheł neso," nee.

"Ggenaa, onee' seyeł tegheedo'," beeznee gheel.

Ts'ʉh, "Oho'," nee.

Kk'ʉdaa eeydee yeł tonołeyo. Kk'ʉdaa yoogh soonhedel'oł dehoon gheelhee. Dehoon kkenaa

He walked and walked and walked, spending the night here and there. He walked for a long time.

He walked along a river, following the bends. When he came around a bend, he saw many people down at the end of a long stretch of the river. He walked toward them. They were playing a game of kickball. Many people were there. The sight was impressive. He went to that place and stood at the edge of where the people were.

A man walked up and said to him, "Friend, did you just arrive?"

"Yes," he said, "I just arrived."

"Come, friend, you will stay with me," the man said to him.

"Okay," K'etetaalkkaanee replied.

He went up the bank with him while the kickball game was going on. They were all talking

aahaa yʉh dohʉdnee yʉh k'ooleeł-tl'onaa, go k'edeeteey netoogh kke-naahedelghus ts'en'.

but he could not understand them, they were talking so fast.

Kk'ʉdaa, "Ggenaa, nʉgh k'etegheehon'," beeznee. Ts'ʉh edeyeł hedonots'eeltaanh.

Then the man said to K'etetaal-kkaanee, "Friend, you will eat," and brought him into his house.

Kk'ʉdaa go hʉn sołt'en yeh daa–dletl'ee. Yoogh kk'ʉdaa k'enaahe-taatlneek. Huyeł hʉn genee ghulaa' go yʉh leggun kk'aant'aay gheel enotaalneek. Huyeł hʉn, "Ggenaa, dzaan yoodʉhte dennots'ehool-'eele," hednee gheel neeł'ehedenee.

Some women were in the house. They began to cook. They were cooking something that looked like dried fish. One of them said to the other, "Friend, we didn't go up to the treetops to do our usual thing."

"Gen koon deloghe te hey'e-laay soo' de'ehednee?" yeneelenh. "Yoogh delogh hʉggaagge hey'e-laay go deheyłneeyee," yeneelenh gheelhee.

K'etetaalkkaanee wondered, "What do they catch in the tree-tops? They must be talking about some game animal that they catch up in the trees," he thought.

Ts'ʉh kk'ʉdaa yʉh k'enolneek. K'egheehon'. Yoogh tledohʉdeel-leyhtl de gheel k'etlekk'aa dent'aa. Bedzoghe dehoot'aa gheelhee. K'egheehon' kk'e de'eełt'aa'aa.

Then the cooking was finished. He ate but not long afterwards he was hungry again. He was hungry. It was as if he had never eaten.

Kk'ʉdaa yoogh henaaldzet. Go ede det'aanh ts'e gheel naaltaanh. Nonługh t'aanh yuh baabc kk'c-hooghee'o. Kk'ʉdaa tlede hʉghee-let. Ts'ʉh ts'aano'eedelet. Huyeł haadok'edeełneeyaa. Kk'ʉdaa kk'odehun' ts'aaneelet. Ts'ʉh doogh hʉneeł'aanh. Huyeł doogh

Then everybody went to bed. As usual, he went to bed. A lot of food was left over. The night passed and he woke up. The house was still when he woke up in the morning. He looked around. Nobody was in the house. When he had gone to bed, the house had been noisy with

hʉn yeh denaa kkelaa. Go t'aanh yʉh kkenaa aahaa yʉh neget ts'e dʉhʉdnee denh. Soot'e yʉh dohʉdnee kk'e dʉhʉdnee tleeteey.

conversation. He thought he heard some noise outside.

Tleeneeyo huyeł denaagheneede dodeggu hʉn koon yʉh tsonggude yeł eł ehon yeł delbegge yeł tl'ogho yʉh hʉdelggʉkk deloghe. At'eeyło eeydee kkaa go yʉgh neeyoyee. Ts'e go k'edeeteey netoogh kkenaa hedelghus ts'e go netoogh koon kk'oheededaał. Ts'ʉh yʉh kk'onk'ehenaadleyeeł kk'e dehet'aanh. Nedaats'e yoogh delbegge ghelgguyhtl te...

He went out and, to his surprise, up on the treetops, willow grouse, spruce grouse, and ptarmigan were all clucking. Those were the people to whom he had come. That was why they had talked so fast and were such fast runners. It had been as if they were flying around. You know how fast ptarmigan are.

Ts'ʉh do'o t'aanh detl'eełten noghoołnook. Ts'ʉh dodoggu yoo ghe yʉhʉ neget ts'e dʉhʉt'aanh k'eełekk'ee nogheek'enh. Eeydee kk'ʉdaa koon enodaadleneege kkaa koon kk'ʉdaa haanodeedeyo.

He picked up his bow and arrow and shot one down from a place where they were all in a group. Strengthened by eating it, he left again.

Tenh Noo K'etełkkʉyenh

The One Who Spears Through the Ice

Ts'e kk'ʉdaa yoogh koon ghehoł, ghehoł. Ts'ʉh go hʉyts'en' hoolaanh ts'ʉh yoogh teey tseetl eełkoghaa gheelhee. Ts'ʉh kk'ʉdaa benh edeeyo. Nedaagh yooghee hʉn ts'o'ʉstl. Eeydee ts'e taalyo. Yeneeł'aanh yets'e ghehoł huyeł yegge hʉn koon k'etełkkʉyh. Huyeł yegge hʉn bebaaney loy hʉn łookk'e hegheghedeełtaanh. Yʉgh neeneeyo.

He walked and walked. Because it was early in the winter, very little snow was on the ground. He came upon a lake. Far across the lake, he saw someone walking. K'etetaalkkaanee started to walk toward him. As he walked toward him, he saw him throwing a spear. A fish hung from his spear when he pulled it from the ice.[1] K'etetaalkkaanee walked up to him.

"Yee'! Ggenaa', zeeduh ent'aa go dest'aanh. Go ees nedudon ghulaa' k'egheson'?" nee, go zee yek'elookk'e neeł'aanh ts'ʉh gheelhee.

"Oh my! Friend, I am just barely walking. I don't know when I ate last," K'etetaalkkaanee said, having seen the man's fish.

Ts'ʉh kk'ʉdaa, "O, enaa seggen'aa', oho', tlaa doogh tl'ee," nee dehoon daa'en bek'ots'e yetaalyo, hodaa. Hʉyeł hʉn go dek'ebaaneyh hʉn taatlkkʉyh. Noyoolneek łookk'e begheghedeełtaanh. At'eeyło "Tenh Noo K'etełkkʉy" beeznee.

The man replied, "Oh, my dear friend, just wait while I get some more." He walked on the ice with K'etetaalkkaanee behind him. They walked slowly and the man threw his spear. A fish hung from it when he pulled it out. Apparently this man is called "The One Who Spears through the Ice."

Kk'ʉdaa łookk'e denloh ts'ʉh kk'ʉdaa nongge yeyeł tonołeyo. Benh ghʉ tobaan yeh hooł'aanh

When the man had caught enough fish, K'etetaalkkaanee went up the bank with him. The man had a

1. The lake was frozen, but the man was able to spear fish through the ice without chopping a hole in it.

łonh de kk'ʉdaa nongge yeyeł hedono'eedeyo. Kk'ʉdaa eet nonł łookk'e yen'eełt'aa'.

house on the shore of the lake. K'etetaalkkaanee went inside with him. The man cooked the fish.

"Ggenaa', k'eehonh," yełnee. Ło'ts'eyʉh k'eenaałdon'. "Ggenaa', neek'edeeghoolkoode yu," yełnee. Ʉhts'e heghe'en yedełnee'aa dehoon.

"Friend, eat some," the man told him. He ate a lot. "Friend, don't save any for later," the man told him, without telling him why he said that.[2]

Łookk'e naałdon' ts'ʉh go hełde debeeznee ts'ʉh doogh k'enot eł t'oh ghee'onh. "Tlaa eey gen ghʉ soo' dednee?" yoodnee ts'en'.

When K'etetaalkkaanee ate, there was so much fish that, in spite of what he had been told, he hid a piece under a spruce bough being used for flooring. He thought, "I wonder why he said that."

Ts'ʉh kk'ʉdaa yoogh hełts'edo-gho ode hoozoonh ts'e tlede hegheelet, hedeggenaa' yeł. Kk'ʉdaa kk'odehun' ts'aaheneelet.

He and his friend visited and then spent a good night together. They woke up in the morning.

Huyeł hʉn, "Hodee ggenaa', benh enozeetot'ustl," beyłnee hʉndenh.

His friend told him, "Okay, friend, let's go out to the lake again."

Go k'ehʉhdeehon' dehoon go neek'edaalkoot.

They had eaten all the food, except what K'etetaalkkaanee had saved.

Gheel kk'ʉdaa notlen nʉkk'ʉ-hedee'ots. Ts'ʉh doogh benotle yohoł. Yeneeł'aanh. Gheel łookk'e taatl-'aanee go ede det'aanh ts'en', go denaa. Huyeł tenh dlet'es.

They walked back down the bank. The man walked ahead of him. K'etetaalkkaanee watched him. The man must have seen a fish, and he began to do what he

2. The man's request was unusual. Food from the evening meal usually was saved for the next morning's meal.

"Yee'! Ggenaa', neek'edaaneenle-koot kk'aant'aa," yełnee.

"Enaa seggen'aa' yʉh baabe kk'aa seyeł hoot'eel k'enaalsdon'. Ts'ʉh łoghʉn k'enot t'aanh neen-s'onh," nee, go zee soohoonaaney deyeeloh eenee'ee.

Ts'ʉh, "Hee! Ggenaa, tonolee-doyh ts'ʉh tledee'oyh," yełnee.

Naa'en denohooloh. Kk'ʉdaa yoonggu tonołeyo. Ts'ʉh tleyede-gheełnenh, go k'enot neeyeenee-'onee. Kk'ʉdaa notlen yʉgh nukk'unodeelggok.

Kk'ʉdaa yoogh koon kk'ok'ehe-naal'eeyh, kk'ok'ehenaal'eeyh. Hu-yeł hʉn kk'ʉdaa koon nok'etaatl-kkʉyh. Huyeł bebaaney loy łookk'e hegheghedeełtaanh. Kk'ʉdaa oho' ts'ʉh kk'ʉdaa nok'ehodon', go łookk'e yenołdlaan nohodon'.

Ts'ʉh kk'ʉdaa, "Ggenaa, o doogh ghesoł," deggenaa' ełnee.

Ts'ʉh, "Oho'," nee. "Enaa segg-en'aa' baasee' go seyeł tlede gheenlet," nee. Hoozoonh ts'e de-ggenaa' yeł tlede gheelet. Ts'ʉh kk'ʉdaa eet koon haanodeedeyo.

usually did. The spear got stuck in the ice. He said, "Oh! My friend, I think you saved some of the food."

"My dear friend, I was not my-self from want of food, and after I filled up, I hid a piece away," K'etetaalkkaanee replied, even though he had done it on purpose.

The man said to him, "Oh dear! Friend, go back up the bank and put it in the fire."

K'etetaalkkaanee rushed back, went back up the bank, and threw the piece of fish that he had saved into the fire. Then he ran back down the bank.

Once again, they were sneaking and sneaking around. Soon the man threw his spear again and pulled up a fish on the end of it. Once again, they ate. They ate the fish that he caught.

Then K'etetaalkkaanee told his friend, "Friend, I have to be going."

His friend said, "Okay. Thank you, my dear friend, for spending the night with me." He had spent a good night with his friend. Once again, he left.

Belaazone
Otter

Yoogh ghehoł, ghehoł, ghehoł. Kk'ʉdaa koon benh ku---h enodeedeyo. Ts'ʉh doogh eet kkokk'e taalyo. Huyeł doogh hʉn yʉh dekenbes oyh yee nehoonolzaah. Dekenbes oyh yee yʉh kkokk'e nosededeyhtl łonh. Go oyh, kk'eeyh eenaadleyoy bekkaal kk'aa hʉyaan' hʉgh eelt'odlee ent'aa go dekenbes oyh. Kkaal ghaałelen gheel go koon dekenbes oyh bets'edegheenee'ee. Grandpa gheelaa' ees ʉh dent'aay ghest'aan' degheenee'.

Ts'ʉh kk'ʉdaa aado kk'ełyee yʉh k'edeeteey hʉts'e nehoonolzaah. Ts'ʉh eet hʉts'e kkokk'e ghehoł. Eet kk'ełyee ghehoł huyeł do'o hʉn hodzonhghee'o. Go hootl'ełts'e hʉdaalkk'un' te gheel go hołeghee'o. Dehoon hodzonhghee'o te hełde yoogh hʉdaałets'eek kk'e dehoot'aa tʉh. Do'o hʉnde hodzonhghee'o. Ts'ʉh doogh go ede det'aanh ts'e łaałdoy neeneeyo. Ts'ʉh dekkaa' dełgheł. Naayegge hedoneeyo. Huyeł donł hʉn koon tlekkun'daadetlaakk. Kk'un' aadelt'aał. Dehoon doogh hʉn saakkaay ggołtl'oyooz kkaa yeh daadletl'ee.

He walked and walked and walked. Again, he came to a very big lake. He walked across the lake. He could see board-snowshoe tracks all around. Many people had been walking back and forth wearing board-snowshoes. They were snowshoes made of birch boards that had been bent up at one end. They are called *dekenbes oyh*. The only lacing was near the foot. My late grandpa said that he had owned snowshoes like that.

K'etetaalkkaanee walked toward the lower end of the lake where there was an outlet, toward where there were still more tracks. He continued to walk on the lake toward the outlet. As he got closer, off to the side he saw steam rising. Usually, when there is a large fire, smoke rises. But this was different; when there is a slow fire, what comes out looks more like steam. Steam was extending upward from the house. As usual, he went up to the entryway, brushed off his feet, and entered. The fireplace had wet wood in it. The wood was hissing. There were children in the house.

Ts'ʉh, "Go ło yʉhdełne kkaa hodee?" hʉłnee.

He asked them, "Where are your parents?"

"Mendon denaahʉdełne een en naahetaałdaatl," hednee.

"Our parents went out hunting early this morning," they replied.

"O! Go ło edenk'e saakkaay edzoo nelaan de ło go tlekkun'-daaneet'aa' denh?" nee gheelhee. Naa'en kk'aaghe tleeno'eedeyo. Kk'ʉdaa do'ooghe yʉh kkun' hoo-laanh. Do'oogh yʉh kkun' degheeł-'aan'. Ts'ʉh kk'ʉdaa eeydee hedo-nodaalyo. Ts'ʉh nonł yʉh tlehʉ-dengheełggut. Hʉdeekk'onh. Ho go t'aanh kkun' aadelt'aał denh. Doogh saakkaay hʉn koon yʉh hedetaałenenh, edzoo aahaa. Dehoon saak'ehedetaatltlaał gheel-hee. Dehoon kk'ʉdaa kk'ʉdaa ee-naadlekooh. Kk'ʉdaa doogh kku-naaghe ledo. O yoogh k'ehonh gheelhee, nedaats'e ghulaa'.

Then he said, "Gosh! Aren't the children cold? There's only wet wood in the fire." He went back outside. There was a lot of dry wood around the house.[1] He cut some of the dry wood, brought it in, and piled it on the fire. The fire started blazing, whereas the wet wood had barely been burning before. Soon the children were shivering from the cold. Their teeth began to chatter. In the meantime he had warmed up. He was sitting by the fire. He must have had something to eat.

Yoogh ode dehoot'aa huyeł hʉn haantoodetaadlelohtl eetl'ekk. Haantoodellohtl. Hʉyeł hʉnde dotlee ben't'oyeh doyehts'e hʉn koon tleghelbaay belo nʉ'ʉndaal'oy hʉn koon yʉh denaa een honaa-ghedledaatl. At'eeyło hebedełne kkaa.

Some time had passed when he suddenly heard the sound of water running off of something. Water was running. By the door-way, out of the *ben't'oyeh*, some people came with grayling in their mouths.[2] Apparently they were the parents.

1. Because the otter people burned only wet wood, dry wood was plentiful near the house.

2. Old underground houses had an area called a *ben't'oyeh* dug out on each side of the entrance to the main room. One side was used as a bathroom, and the other as a pantry. In the otter house, these areas led into the creek.

Nonł go tleghelbaay hʉts'e hetaatldaatl. Dehoon, "Haa! Go ło nedaats'e hʉgh saakaay hʉdeedeteeyh denh?" Notlee koon too nenoholtluh. Ts'ʉh noyeh haatodellohtl eetl'ekk. Huyeł hʉn dotleets'e hʉn koon kkun' tseł yeł koon kk'ʉdaa honohodedaatl. Nonł yʉh kkun' zoo' hʉydekk'oyh de yʉh eeydee tleeghoheyedaaltlaakk. Haanokkundaadlet'aał. Haadelt'aał.

They threw down the fish and said, "Hey! Why are the children freezing?" They jumped back into the water where they had come up. He heard the water sloshing down below. They came back up with some wet wood. They piled it on top of the good wood that was burning. Once again it started to hiss.

Dehoon go tleghelbaay enaahetlneek gheelhee. Kk'ʉdaa go eeydee naahetaałdon'. Eeydee yennoheedon'. Dehoon nooyoogh tl'ee k'eldlo.

They cooked the grayling and everyone began to eat. They ate the grayling. More were lying there.

Yoogh odzoo aahaa yʉh naal taanh gheelhee. Eet letaanh. Huyeł hʉn yoogh tlede hʉgheelet. Yʉh yenhedeeltloł go yeh daadletl'eey kkaa t'aanh dehoon gheel beł eenaadledaakk.

He was so cold that he went to bed. He lay there. Before he knew it, the night had passed. He had gone to sleep listening to these people snorting with their noses.[3]

Yoogh nedaats'e noholeł huyeł gheel ts'aano'eedelet. Huyeł kk'ʉdaa ts'aaneelet. Haadok'edeełneeyaa. Hʉneeł'aanh. Huyeł doogh hʉn k'ekkelaa. Ts'e hogho doogh go doogh henaaldzet yeneelenh t'aanh hu hʉneeł'aanh. Doogh zo k'ekkel dehoon donługh zo yʉh ekee hʉdeełt'aa, et'eeyło yʉh hʉk'en aahaa.

He did not know how much time had passed before he woke up. He woke up. The house was quiet. He looked around. Everyone was gone. He looked over at the place where he thought they should have been sleeping. The floor was all messy, apparently with their excrement.

3. Otters exhale loudly while breathing normally.

Belaazon ... go gen ghʉ ghulaa' go sołt'en kkaa hełde koon belaazon dełnee'aa dehoon bezeye hednee ts'ʉhʉyaan'. Go hełde ts'ohoołtlaagge. Heyłnee deheghe'en eeydaa' hełde denaak'esaakkaay bekk'e detot'aa'. O yoogh beyeege hoolaanh ts'e huyeł gheelhee. Denaak'esaakkaay bekk'e detot'aan' ts'e ts'ohootołtlaagge heyłnee. Deheghe'en hełde sołt'en kkaa k'oheyeneeghee'enh. Sołt'en kkaa yeghotlee'etlk'elaa. K'eełʉgh koon heyeleł detllaaghe yoogh kk'ʉdaa kk'aahooneełtaanh kk'aant'aay yaan' koon yeleł dełlaah go ʉhts'e heghe'ene.

I don't know why it is, but women are not supposed to use the word *belaazone*; they say *bezeye* instead.[4] It may be because otters have bad toilet habits. If we call an otter by its name, our children will have that problem. Also, otters have some spirit power. Our children may become like that and have bad toilet habits. That is why they kept otters away from women. Women never skinned them. That is also why women never tanned the hide until after they had stopped bearing children.[5]

Ts'ʉhʉ donłʉgh go t'aanh tlekkun'daaneet'aa' gheelhee. Ts'ʉh kk'ʉdaa naa'en kkun' okko tleeneeyo. Ts'ʉh kk'ʉdaa tl'ogho yʉh hʉdeełkk'onh. At'eeyło bezey enheldlaat. K'enhetllaat. Ts'ʉh too nehʉhʉngheełyoot gheelhee. Ts'e ło go k'ekkelaa. Ts'ʉh go tleghelbaay heyogho k'egheehon kkaa gheel ts'aaneelet. Eet hʉdeegheełkk'un'. Ts'ʉh kk'ʉdaa eeydee kkaa koon kk'ʉdaa k'ehetllaat. Ts'ʉh yʉh eet koon kk'ʉdaa haanodeedeyo.

K'etetaalkkaanee looked at the place where the wood had been sizzling. He went back outside to get some dry wood. Then he built a fire outside. Apparently they had turned into otters. They had been transformed and had all gone into the water. That is why no one was around. He ate the leftover grayling for breakfast and kept the fire burning for a while. Like the others, they had been transformed. Once again, he left.

4. *Belaazone* and *bezeye* are both *Denaakk'a* words for otter. *Beleezone* means "one whose hands are bad." *Bezeye* means "shiny black one."

5. Otters snort and have warts on their paws. Women feared that their children would be born with these undesirable characteristics. Children were not allowed to touch otter paws because the parents feared that they might get warts.

Tseyaa Nʉgh Neso
Grandpa, I Have Come to You

Kk'ʉdaa koon yoogh ghehoɫ, ghehoɫ, ghehoɫ. Kk'ʉdaa yoogh nedaats'e neenok'eedeyo. Kk'ʉdaa koon go ede det'aanh ts'e go benh ghʉ kkokk'e neno'eho'. Ts'ʉh koon benh enodeedeyo. Huyeɫ hʉn yegge hʉn yoonee taakk'aatl'o hʉn ts'elhaanh de hʉn hʉtaatl-'aanh. Ts'ʉh eet hʉts'e kkokk'e gheeyo. Ts'ʉh kk'ʉdaa yʉgh neeghehoɫ. Do'o hʉn koon taageɫtlts'etl-'onh. Yʉgh neeneeyo. Huyeɫ go hʉn tseek'aal nelaanh gheelhee ts'e go.

He walked and walked and walked. He walked for a long time. As usual, he came to a lake and proceeded to walk across it. He came to another lake. He could see somebody standing at the upper end of the lake. He walked across the lake toward him. As he was approaching him, he saw that the person was fishing with a hook through a hole in the ice. He walked up to him. It was an old man.

"Setseyaa, nʉgh neso," yeɫnee eehoo. "Setseyaa, go ees nʉgh neso," yeɫnee eehoo.

And so K'etetaalkkaanee said, "Grandpa, I have come to you," but nothing happened. "Grandpa, I have come to you," he said again. Nothing happened.

Taageɫtl-'etl-'onh. Edenk'e nek'e k'e'elaaghee? Kk'ʉdaa koon, "Setseyaa, nʉgh neso," yeɫnee eehoo. "Setseyaa, nʉgh neso," koon yenodednee eehoo. Taageɫtl-'etl-'onh. "Tseyaa, nʉgh neso," nee dehoon yʉh yeyehnaadletl'eɫ.

The old man just continued to fish through the ice. Didn't he ever catch anything? K'etetaal-kkaanee said to him again, "Grandpa, I have come to you," but to no avail. Once again, he repeated, "Grandpa, I have come to you." The old man just sat there fishing. "Grandpa, I have come to you," K'etetaalkkaanee said, and then he butted the old man with his head.

No'o yʉh degge nodaadlenenh. Degge daanoneełtset. Taagełtl-'etl-'onh.

Kk'ʉdaa ło'ts'eyʉh yedodende-neyh. "Setseyaa, nʉgh neso," nee eehoo.

Kk'ʉdaa doyoolaah. Ts'e nedaanh k'edee yʉh bekonh hʉdetaadlenenh ts'e go yʉh yegełtl kk'aa yʉh taaghedetseetl. Degełdle tl'ooł ghʉ eetent'uk de-hoon, "Bezo mendon yoonoogh nʉhʉtset," nee.

Kk'ʉdaa ło'ts'eyʉh, "Tseyaa, nʉgh neso," nee eehoo. Yedode-naałeneek. Go eeydee hełde edo-denaałeneek. Yeyeł tlede eelelaa. Ʉhts'e heghe'en hełde koon yoogh neełyeł kkenaahedelghus eehoo eenh nedaats'e nooyoogh et'eghł saakkaay dent'aa eehoo k'ets'ets'e heyeneehedeelaanh. Ʉhts'e heghe'en hełde koon, "Onts'aa yʉh 'Tseyaa, Nʉgh Neso'" hednee.

Ts'ʉh doo' edeehoo' yʉgh haa-nodeedeyo. Yedodenaałeneek. Eet hełde kk'ʉdaa nedaats'e hʉden'aa' ghulaae' go koon yekk'e taalyo eet hełde kk'ʉdaa tlede gheelet bezełnee'aa.

The old man fell over, jumped back up, and started fishing through the ice again.

K'etetaalkkaanee could not get a response. "Grandpa, I have come to you," he kept saying in vain.

K'etetaalkkaanee did not know what to do, but conveniently, he got a stomachache and defecated into the water hole. Finally, the old man cleaned his line and said, "Ah, no wonder the sun rose differ-ently this morning."

K'etetaalkkaanee said, "Grand-pa, I have come to you," but he still got no response. He could not get the old man to reply. That time he got absolutely no response so he did not spend the night with him. That is why, to this day, when people are talking to each other and one of them is not listening—you know how young people are nowadays, you talk to them and they never listen—people will say of that person, "Just like 'Grandpa, I Have Come to You.'"

He left the man. He could not get any response from him. I don't even know what kind of person that man was. K'etetaalkkaanee just passed him by. That man was one with whom he did not spend the night.

Negoodzeghe
Horned Owl

Ts'ʉh kk'ʉdaa yoogh ghehoł, ghehoł, ghehoł. Kk'ʉdaa yoogh nedaats'e neenok'eedeyo. Doogh hełts'en' hetseghełdaaneelo dehoon ts'ebaa laał kkaakenh te ghehoł. Huyeł hʉnde do'ots'e hʉnde koon deyh bete k'edetaal'oy doteel ghehoł. "Haa! Enaa seggen'aa', kk'ʉdaa yʉh denaateltl-'eey de dogheet'aa' koon det'aanh?" deggenaa' ełnee eehoo. Dehoon beyeneeł'aanh dehoon tson yeneełenh kk'aant'aa. Ts'ʉh, "Denaa zoo'," yoodnee. O, go yek'edeyh neeł'aanh. Ts'uh gheel, "Ggenaa, doogh edʉghʉ ts'ʉhʉdeetolkk'oł hu tlede soleł," yełnee.

Huyeł hʉnde yent'oyh ts'ʉhʉyaan'.

Ts'ʉh, "O, go ło hełaage," yoodnee. Ts'ʉh kk'ʉdaa doogh neehʉhdaaneetlaatl. Kkun' ghʉ neełk'ots'enh yeh neek'ehedaalyo. Degheel kk'ʉdaa tlede hetoleł de neehenee'ots. Go deyh bete k'edetaal'oy nonł yʉh ekkʉneek'egheełtleyh. Kk'ʉdaa nonł eeydee et'aał. Yeyeł henaayh huyeł hʉnde

He walked and walked and walked along. He had walked a long time. It was dusk and he was walking among some big spruce trees. Somebody was walking toward him, carrying some spruce grouse on a stick. K'etetaalkkaanee said to his friend, "Oh, my dear friend, how long has it been since I've seen another person?" but his friend did not answer. K'etetaalkkaanee looked at him and he appeared to be smiling. "Well, he looks friendly," K'etetaalkkaanee thought. He looked at the spruce grouse. "Well, friend, I guess we can make a fire near here and spend the night."

The man just nodded.

K'etetaalkkaanee thought, "Oh, okay, this person must not be able to speak." They cut some spruce boughs to sit on and lie on, and they made places across the fire from each other. They settled down to spend the night. They took the spruce grouse that were on the stick and put them over the

heɫaage ts'e yekk'aa'eelneek. Ts'ʉh neyeenaatlneyh. Dehoon yekk'oye-neek'eeɫleet, "Donts'e hʉn belo hʉkkelaa. Bentseyh yeɫ benogh yeɫ k'ehoolaanh."

Kk'ʉdaa nonɫ eeydee k'eghʉn-ɫet'aa'. Huyeɫ hʉnde deggenaa' ts'e nonaan noyedaaneetonh. Ts'ʉh, "Seyaan' teghesonee? Nedaats'e hʉgh seeyaan' taagheson go denɫ-'aanee," yeɫnee. Go k'etseɫtlen' haa-deneeɫk'eɫ. Eeydee yets'e ghe'oɫ.

Huyeɫ nonɫ kkun' ts'e teɫneyh. At'eeyɫo kk'ʉdaa haahaa k'ehonh ts'e gheelhee. Ts'ʉh go dezaay yʉh yeɫ nonaan yets'e no'eeltluh. Ts'ʉh go belo hootolaa' eehu yoodnee de yʉh hootltsut.

"Enaa seggenaa'!" daadeyoh. Saakk aahaa yuhu notaaltset dehoon, "Enaa seggenaa' selo hootltseenh," detaalnee'. Ts'ʉh go naa'ts'e koon bʉgh yeet'aan ts'e yekk'aa'eelneegee ts'e go naa'ts'e koon yeetltsut beeznee.

My! Hʉn koon k'etaalhon'

fire. The spruce grouse were roasting. K'etetaalkkaanee talked to this person, realizing that he could not speak. The man made signs to him. K'etetaalkkaanee was thinking, "That man has no mouth, although he has a nose and eyes."

The spruce grouse finished cooking, and the man passed the stick across to him. K'etetaalkkaanee said to him, "Am only I to eat? How can I eat this all by myself?" He tore off one wing with some meat and offered it to the man.

The man pointed to the fire. Apparently that was the way he ate.[1] Then K'etetaalkkaanee grabbed his knife and jumped across the fire to him and made a cut where he thought the man's mouth ought to be.

Suddenly, the man said, "Oh, my dear friend!" K'etetaalkkaanee rubbed saliva on the cut and the man said, "Oh, my dear friend made a mouth for me." K'etetaalkkaanee must have found out that the man did not have a hole in the rear either, and it is said that he made a hole for him there too.

My! The man began to eat.

1. The man ate by burning his food.

et'eeyło belo hʉkkelaa. Ts'ʉh henaayh tʉh neładobaan'ts'enaaltonh dehoon ts'ehenaayh kk'aadenee. Really yʉh daats'e yʉh dent'aa dehoon henaayh. Yʉh belo dok'edaaltuts kk'aadenee. Ʉhts'e gheel hehoonaalhaak eehoo hee.

Apparently he had had no mouth before. That is why the owl talks with its lips pressed together. It really speaks like this.[2] It sounds as if it has something stuffed into its mouth. That is the way it speaks.

My, ło'ts'eyʉh beyeł yehetaalhaak. Go deyh bete k'edetaal'oy kkaa tlede hegheelet. Hełts'edogho k'ehehaaneeyo. Ts'ʉh kk'ʉdaa yoogh beł heenaadledaakk gheelhee.

My! The man began to speak with him. They spent the night there, strengthened by the spruce hens. They talked all evening and fell asleep.

De koon kk'ʉdaa ts'aaneelet. Huyeł go ede dehoot'aa ts'e haadok'edeełneeyaa. Ts'ʉh doogh hunool'aanh huyoł gonoo zokk'uł dehoon yeetlkkonh. Nedaa aay'oo hʉn koon negoodzeghe. At'eeyło negoodzeghe laaghe gheelhee. Hʉn koon doldo ts'ʉhʉyaan'. Ts'ʉh eet koon kk'ʉdaa hʉgh haanozee'ots. At'eeyło koon nodeneeyee, nodeneeyee laaghe koon beeznee.

He woke up in the morning. As usual, there was no noise. He looked around and did not see anyone; it was daylight. An owl was sitting up on a tree nearby. Apparently that man had been meant to become a great horned owl. It was the only thing in the area, sitting up there on the tree. Once again, K'etetaalkkaanee left. That bird is also known as *nodeneeyee*.[3]

---

2. Catherine Attla spoke with her lips pressed together while she said this sentence.

3. *Nodeneeyee* means "the one who foretells the future." The horned owl might predict something bad by saying, *"Tegheetsaeh,"* "You are going to cry," or it might foretell something good by saying, *"Nek'etsaah bede tohłggooł,"* "You guys will crunch the belly meat of something," which means that the person hearing it will be lucky in catching game.

Sooge
Marten

Ts'ʉh koon kk'ʉdaa yoogh ghehoł. Kk'ʉdaa eey dehoon hʉyh neets hʉkk'e neeholeł, neek'ohoł. Kk'ʉdaa hʉyh neets hukk'e neek'e-neeyo. Doogh ghehoł, ghehoł. Ts'ʉh doogh yoogh noo yekk'e gheel gheholee.

Once again, he was walking along. It was almost midwinter; he had been walking that long. He had walked until midwinter. He walked and walked. He was walking through the woods.

Huyeł hʉnde yooneets'e hʉts'e bekk'e hʉnde, "Hʉdee---yh! Dont'aa doogh nok'eedeyo łonh. Bekk'aa'ʉhdaał, bekk'aa'ʉhdaał," ts'edetaalnee' eetl'ekk.

Behind him, someone said, "Hey! Something walked around here. Follow it, everybody, follow it," he heard someone say.

Ts'ʉh, "Hʉ gen soo' koon ded-nee nedaats'e hʉden'aa' dednee?" yeenaaldleen'. Ts'ʉh kk'ʉdaa ho-nodeneeyo neełlot hu. Ts'ʉh dekk'e hʉkk'e donołeyo. Ło'ts'e bekk'e yooneets'e hʉts'en', yooneets'e hʉ-ts'en'. Bekk'e dozołneyhtl eetl'ekk.

He thought, "What is that? What kind of person is that?" He walked in a big circle and came back to where he had started. While he was doing that, he could hear the man following him and talking.

"Nʉgh ees deten hʉkk'e donołeyo," ts'ednee eetl'ekk. "Bʉgh dek'ʉhtl'ooh."

He heard him say, "It came back to its own tracks. Set a snare for it, fellas."

Kkʉnobeyedeenaalyo. Kk'ʉdaa eet kkʉnobeyedenohoł, kkʉnobe-yedenohoł. "Nedaats'e hʉgh hoye-neetʉhłleet."

The marten began following K'etetaalkkaanee around in a circle. He followed him and followed him. "Don't ruin[1] it, fellas."

1. He is concerned that by chasing the marten, the meat will be ruined.

Doogh hʉn k'eełekk'enh yaan' bekk'e ghehoł łonh go deten hʉkk'e donołeyo denh.

It looked as if only one person's tracks were following him when K'etetaalkkaanee came back on his own tracks.

"Nedaats'e hʉgh hʉyeneetʉhł-leet. Nʉgh k'eełʉgh bʉgh dek'ʉh-tl'ooh," ts'edetaalnee' eetl'ekk. Kk'ʉdaa yoolaatltl'onh. Ts'ʉh yoogh ledo ts'ʉh kk'ʉdaa dehoon kk'eeyh tl'otsets gheel det'aage ye-kk'e daaltleyh. Ts'ʉh yoogh kk'oye-daalkoode gheel k'ek'ʉh yedzoghe hogho neenee'onh. Dehoon yʉh go dek'ek'etseghel de'aak gheel yʉh denaa kk'e denloh.

"Don't ruin it, fellas. Set a snare for it quickly," he heard the voice say. He listened to it. Then it sounded as if it had stopped, so K'etetaalkkaanee took off his parka and stuck a rotten birch log up into it. He put into the chest area some fat that he had been carrying. He made the marten parka look like a man.

"Hodee! Bekk'aano'ʉhdedaał," beeznee. Kk'ʉdaa yooneets'e hʉts'e koon eetl'ekk. Naa'en go ede det'aanh ts'e honodeneeyo. Huyeł go hʉnde dek'ełetl'oonh. Ts'ʉh go kk'eeyh tl'otsets yeyee degheetleey yeyee ek'egheełtleyh. Dehoon k'etleedzodze nelaanh ts'e aadeggu ts'ebaa loghe donaaldo.

"Okay, fellas, start following it again," the voice said. Once again, K'etetaalkkaanee heard the man following him. Again, he walked in a big circle. K'etetaalkkaanee came to the snare and into it he put the parka that he had stuffed with rotten birch. Then he turned himself into a hawk owl and landed on a nearby spruce tree.

Kk'ʉdaa yooneets'e hʉts'e nots'ot'ustl eetl'ekk. Yʉh ło'ts'eyʉh kk'odozaalneeyh gheelhee go ts'ehenaayh ts'en'.

Then he heard the man coming closer. Wherever the man went, K'etetaalkkaanee could clearly hear him talking constantly.

Do'o hʉnde kk'ʉdaa ggaabeeł t'o ts'etltaanh. "Yeey! Yaadeheye-laah. Dotoneeł heyłneey go yʉh

There it was in the snare! The man said, "My goodness! Why didn't they do that in the first

hʉyeneeheyedetaadleledee," nee. No'o bʉgh neets'enee'ots. Ts'ʉh go bedzoghe yʉh ts'ehootlkk'ʉyh, saay aahaa. K'ek'ʉh neełkk'aaneegheł. Ts'ʉh kk'ʉdaa "Oho', tlaat. Tlaatlaa, tlaa nekk'aa'. Tlaa nekk'aa' dehoon kk'ʉdaa neenʉhnaayh."

place? What were they doing, ruining it?" The man went over to it. He split the chest open with a knife. The fat fell apart. Then he said, "Okay, wait. Let it cool off. Let it cool off, and let's make camp."

Yʉh tl'ogho yʉh beyeł kk'ots'edenaadeggoode kk'aadnee. Denaa k'eełekk'ee yaan' eenee'ee. Kk'ʉdaa no'o ło'ts'eyʉh tlʉhʉdegheetlaatl. Ts'ʉh go zeetoltl'ee nee hʉyeł yʉh go kkunaaghe neehoneetleyh. "Tlaa gutl dʉhghonh, tlaa hoozoonh ts'e nekk'aa'. Nedaats'e hʉgh bʉgh enaahto," ts'ednee edeyełnozednee gheelnee. Dehoon kk'ʉdaa gutl laaghe kk'ʉdaa do'ooghe dekenh kk'ʉdaa degheeł'aan'. "Gon hełde k'ekkaa' bet'o tot'aalee, gon hełde k'elo' gutl, gon hełde k'etlee' gon hełde k'eledle', gon koon k'eledle', gon hełde k'etl'eele', gon koon k'etl'eele'." Kk'ʉdaa nedaats'e neek'egheetaałeno'.

He talked as if many people were with him, even though he was the only one there. Then the man cut a big pile of wood. Then he made places around the fire for people to sit. "Okay, fellas, now make some cooking sticks while it's cooling. There's no reason to rush things," he said, talking to himself. Then he got some sticks and began to sharpen them. "This one is going to be for cooking the foot. This stick is for the hand, this one for the head, this one for the hind leg, this one for the other hind leg, this one for the arm, and this one for the other arm." He did this for a long time.

Ts'ʉh go gutl deghonh dehoon no'o k'etleedzodze doldoy tleedonok'endedluh. "Heee'! Enaa k'edekule k'etaagheson' yeneelen ło do'o dedneeyee?" yełnee. Et'eeyło koon ʉdenh go deyłnee.

While the man made cooking sticks, the hawk owl sat up in the tree, laughing. The man said, "Oh, that poor thing. Is it laughing because it thinks it is going to eat?" He did not realize that he was talking to K'etetaalkkaanee.

Ʉhts'e heghe'en ent'aa yegge,

That is why people these days

"Onts'aa k'etleedzodze k'etltaanh." Dotson' gheel eey yoogh not'ʉhtl te yʉh eeydee kk'e donodeneel-tl'eyhtl dehoon tleedonok'ende-dluh kk'aadnee. Yegge ees ʉhts'e heghe'ene ts'ednee, go k'etleedzo-dze k'egheeɫtaa'. Ts'e go ʉdenh koon k'eyeetltaanh. Koon tl'ee ʉhts'e heghe'ene. Go delk'ehoo ees k'edeeteey yeetltaanh. Tl'ogho yʉh delk'ehoo yʉgh tleedonok'ende-dluh dehoon yekk'e donodeneel-tl'eyhtl. Zʉhge koon yeetltaanh hednee. Go ʉdenh dedegheenee' ts'en'. Ts'ʉh, "Onts'aa koon k'etlee-dzodze k'etltaanh," hednee. Go eet k'egheeɫtaa' deheghe'ene.

say, "Just like a hawk owl," when someone teases others. That is also why the raven teases the hawk owl while it flies. It swoops down over the hawk owl and makes noises like laughter. It is because of what the hawk owl did in this story. It teased someone. Other birds also tease the hawk owl because of that. The robin teases it the most. The robin will laugh at it and tease it. It will fly towards it as if to hit it and then fly off again. They say that the camp robber is another one that does that. It is the hawk owl's own fault because it teased the marten. People will say, "Just like the hawk owl that teased that person," because of the hawk owl's behavior in this story.

Yʉgh tleedonok'endedluh.

K'etetaalkkaanee laughed and laughed at the man.

Kk'ʉdaa k'ekkokk'e neeɫk'ots'en koonh. Kk'ʉdaa hʉn k'ekonh koonh. "Gon heɫde k'edzaaye' gon heɫde k'edzaadeelo' gon heɫde k'ekole'one, gon heɫde k'eggol-dzeede'." Nedaats'e yoogh yʉh ne-notsʼeghenaaɫeyonh tsʼe detlekts'e yʉh gutl hʉte detaalghʉnh. Kk'ʉ-daa dehoon yʉh kkunaaghe yʉh hʉ-neenyedaaltleyh, go ts'eghʉɫdenh.

Then the man made sticks for each side of ribs and one for the stomach too. "This is going to be for the heart, this one for the lungs, this one for the liver, and this one for the kidneys." He made sticks for every part of the body. Then he planted them all around the fireplace and got everything ready.

Kk'ʉdaa gutl degheeghonh

After he finished making the

łoghʉne. Ts'ʉh, "Nedaaghe hełde kk'eł neenotohdedeyhtl?" nee. Ts'ʉh kk'ʉdaa aa'en neetleehʉnaal-'aatl. De daa'en ts'ebaa deenaatl-ghaats, eeydee baalyo. De daa'en kenee ghedetotl koon kk'ʉdaa. Ahu koon kk'ʉdaa hebaano'oodeetaał-dok. Ʉhts'e gheel go heghe'en ts'e-baa tleekk'e bʉgh haał ledlo hee. Naa'en ts'ebaa yedeenaatlghaadze koon baalyo. Kk'ʉdaa kk'aaghe ehu koon neełloy nenoltlek. Ts'ʉh no'o kkunaaghe neenoltlek.

sticks, he said, "Where are you fellas going to relieve yourselves?" Then he broke a trail over to a spruce tree. He knocked down the spruce tree and walked its length on top of it. Then he jumped into the snow and rolled around. Then he jumped back on the spruce tree and began to walk back and forth on it. That is why people set traps for marten on spruce trees that have fallen. He knocked down another spruce tree and walked to the end of it. Then he began to go back and forth from tree to tree. He came back to the fireplace.[2]

Ts'ʉh, "Hodee, kk'ʉdaa?" Kk'ʉdaa tson' kk'aatoey koon hoo-dletseenh. "Oho', kk'ʉdaa nʉ'ʉhł-'ʉhtl kk'ʉdaa neenʉht'oł." Kk'ʉdaa naangge bʉgh neenots'eet'ots. Go yʉh ts'etlkk'ʉyh ts'e yʉh dent'aa go k'ekʉh. Eet donłe kk'ʉdaa be-nolozaadleleyh. Go kk'ʉdaa benołełdeetaaghtlkeł beeznee dehʉghuʉnh. Hʉn koon kk'eeyh tl'otsets neełkk'aaneegheł. Yeneeł-'aanh, yeneeł'aanh. Go hʉn kk'eeyh tl'otsets yaan' beyee kkokk'e de-ghee'o. Hedodegheetset. "Hmh! Hmh!" detaalnee'. Notlen go hʉdeetokk'oł denh neenots'eet'ots.

Then he said, "Okay, fellas, are you ready?" The toilet had been made. "Okay, fellas, butcher what we caught. Cut it up now." The chest was cut in half, and the fat was visible. He went back over to it. He thrust the knife deep into it and cut downwards towards the stomach in order to skin it. He cut into it and the rotten birch fell apart in two pieces. He looked and looked at it. The only thing in the parka was a rotten birch log. He stopped talking. Then he started saying "Hmh! Hmh!" Quietly, he walked back over to the fireplace.

2. He had knocked down the trees to make a path across the snow to the toilet. The place where he rolled in the snow was the toilet.

Eet ts'ʉhʉneeł'aanh. Huyeł nonłe haakkun'zaaneełtleyh.

He looked at it. Then he lit the fire.

Doogh, "Yee! Nedaanh henaaghedoodeneeyh?" nee. Go hełde koon yegge donłe' bet'o yoot'aal edeenh daa', go k'enohʉdeetodedlook, k'edeeteey gheelhee. Dehe'en gheel go ghulaa', "Yee! Nedaadenh henaaghdoodeneeyh?" nee dehoon denaan' aahʉdeneet'otl. Saakk aahaa yuhu notaaltset dehoon neeyeeneedzenh. Ts'ʉh kk'ʉdaa gutl deghenaalt'aa' ts'e detlekts'e hʉloghe hʉte yeghenaaltlt'aa'. Dehoon kk'ʉdaa nonłe yʉh hʉdeekk'onh.

He said, "Oh dear! Where can we cut off a piece of ourselves next?" He said that because if he were to leave the sticks there without cooking anything on them, there would be too much starvation in the future. Saying, "Yee! Where can we cut off a piece of ourselves next?" he cut a piece of meat from his own face. He rubbed with saliva the place from which he had cut the piece, and it healed. Then he diced the piece he had cut off. He put a piece on each cooking stick. The fire began to blaze while he did that.

Kk'ʉdaa, "Haa'! Haa'!" detaalnee'. "Hʉdokk'oł eetl'ekk! Hʉdokk'oł eetl'ekk!" Kkun' teł notaadletlek. Kkun' teł notaadletlek. Huyeł gutl k'eełekk'ee beyekk'e daadledok. Hʉkk'aay taadletlʉh. Ts'ʉh gutl gho eeltluh, eeydee bʉgh daalgok. Naa'en hʉnde koon sooge deydle kuh haadeeltluh. Naa'en go ts'ebaa tleekk'e neełloy neghel-tlek hu daa'en t'aanh haadeel tluh.

Then he said, "Listen! Listen! A forest fire is coming! A forest fire is coming!" He began to jump back and forth over the fire. He jumped back and forth over it. Suddenly, he was pierced by one of the cooking sticks. He landed short and was impaled on it. A big male marten left that place. It took off, running on the trees upon which the man had walked back and forth.

Nełtseeł
Wolverine

Ts'ʉh kk'ʉdaa yoogh koon ghehoł, ghehoł, ghehoł. Kk'ʉdaa nedaats'e neenok'eedeyo. Huyeł hʉn doogh hʉn ts'eneeno łonh. Doogh ehu denaa kk'e taalyo. Doogh ehu ghehoł. Huyeł go hʉn ggaagge kkenh ghedetlaatl łonh. Ts'ʉh go eet hʉneeł'aanh. O yoogh k'etlekk'aa gheel baabe okko hʉneeł'aanee. Ts'ʉhʉ doogh zeeyʉh eet lehaanh dehoon doogh hʉneeł'aanh. Nedaa do'o hʉn yʉh nełtseeł ghoo' kkenh kk'e dol'onh.

Once again, he walked and walked and walked. He had been walking for a long time again. He came upon a trail that looked as if people had been moving on it. He began to follow the people. He walked on their trail. Then he came to a place where someone had been chopping on a beaver lodge. He looked at it. He might have been hungry and looking for food. He stood there and looked around. There was a wolverine's tooth lying on the lodge.

"Hʉdaa! Koon dogheet'aa'ee?" yeneelenh. "O, go ło eeydee go kkenh gheetlaadlee taaltlaatl eehu łonee," yeneelenh. Ts'ʉh yoolneek. Ts'ʉh yoogh dehaałlel yee yeghee'onh. Ts'ʉh doogh ehu ghehoł. Ts'eneeno łonh hu ghehoł.

He thought, "Hmm, I wonder where that came from." Then he thought, "Oh, maybe he was the one who started to chop the beaver lodge, then quit." He took the tooth and put it in his pack. He followed the trail. He kept following the trail on which the people had traveled.

Huyeł donł hʉn kk'ʉdaa hʉdaalkk'un'. Ts'ʉh gheel kk'ʉdaa eet kkun' gho neeyo. Doogh neeneeyo. Ts'ʉh et'eeyło go hʉn bedenaa' kkaa lonh. Sołt'en kkaa koonh yeh daadletl'ee. Eet gheel hedoneeyo hee. Yoogh kkun' aaneeyo gheelhee.

Then he saw a fire up ahead, and he went to the camp. He stopped there. It was a family with many children. Some women were also staying there. He entered the house and sat down by the fire.

Huyel hun, "Nugh neeyonenh oho k'eno'ohlneyhtl!" ts'ednee. Kk'udaa nonle solt'en kkaa baabe ghu kk'otaaleneek.

The man said, "Cook something for the visitor!" Then the women began to cook.

Dehoon go solt'aanh k'eele-kk'enh gheel, "Yeey! Yuhtsey ent'aa nugh betlaatleel ehoolne-ghee," nee. "Yendenaa'eeldleen' ent'aa nughunee," ts'ednee.

One of the women said, "Your grandpa there just broke his axe. That person will starve us," she said.[1]

Kk'udaa heyek'egheelon'. Et'eeylo debedetaaghsnee' yelnee dehugh go, "Neeyonenh oho k'eno'ohlneytl," nee go denaa.

They fed him and he ate. The man wanted to ask a favor of him and that is the reason he had said, "Cook something for the visitor."

Kk'udaa k'egheehon'. Ts'e doogh ledo.

K'etetaalkkaanee ate and sat around.

Huyel hun, "Dotoneel go nee-ts'e tlaatleel ent'aa go seyel behool-neghee. Baadenh dohutoneelee?" nee koon kk'udaa, udenh.

"What are we going to do about this axe that's been in the family so long? It broke on me. What are we going to do without it?" the man asked.

Huyel hun, "Haa! Duhudnee denh. Hmn! Dzaan eneets'e ghesol de go hun kkenh ghedetlaatl lonh. Go hun eet neltseel ghoo' dol'onh."

"Oh! Now that you mention it, when I was walking today, I came upon a beaver lodge that someone had been chopping on. I found a wolverine tooth there."

Kk'udaa, "Hu! Adenk'e see lo nugh yeh detseelee selnee? See

"Hm! Is it me that he is calling 'the one who messes his bed and

1. The woman was speaking indirectly of "Grandpa," her husband. She meant that because he could not hunt, he could not provide food for his family. The women in this story are the Wolverine Man's wives.

ent'aa eey neełneggʉde yoo ghʉ tlen tleehoontltluh. Go baabe aahaa yʉh hebetlen haa kk'e dehoot'aa hʉłnee ts'e gheelhee. Go hʉtaadle'o ts'e sołt'en ek'etlłonh nee ts'en'. De daa'en dodnee ghulaa'.

clothing?'[2] I am the person who keeps the path from the door of my wives' house yellow." What he meant was that he provided for his wives so well that the path was yellow with grease. That was his way of saying that he fed his wives well. He said more after that.

"E! Hʉnedaats'e go hełde dehaasnee. Kk'ʉdaa yʉh k'etlekk'aa seyeł hoot'aan denh," koon nodednee. Ts'ʉh kk'ʉdaa yetl'onoyeghee'onh łoghʉne.

K'etetaalkkaanee said, "Oh! What am I talking about? I'm not myself because I'm hungry." He gave the tooth to the man.

Ts'ʉh kk'ʉdaa, "Tlaa tlaa zo dotoneeł? Tlaa nʉgh zee eetengheeł'aan'," beeznee.

The man said, "What good is it to me like this? Why don't you just look at it, even if you might not be able to fix it?"

"Oho', go see zo dotaaghsleeł dʉhʉghʉnh? Hʉ nedaats'e hogho desehednee. Nełten dʉkk'ʉghʉn'esluk de ent'aa gonh," nee. Go saahooltsoł nee ts'en'.

"Okay, but I don't know how I can fix it if you can't. I'm the person known for snapping the thunder with a snare," K'etetaalkkaanee said. That was his way of saying that he was too strong to work on a small thing such as the wolverine's axe.[3]

"Hʉ! Ts'e zo dotoneeł? O tlaa

"Well, what good is it to me

2. The word for wolverine, ***nełtseeł***, sounds like the word ***nedetseeł***, which means "he has continuous diarrhea." In general, it is considered disrespectful to refer to a powerful animal by its name, so circumlocutions are often used. Nowadays, a wolverine is usually called ***doyonh*** "chief" or, by women, ***tł'onyee*** "parka border trimming."

3. K'etetaalkkaanee was teasing the wolverine man. He acted humble by saying that he did not know how to fix the tooth, but he also bragged about his strength and power. When he said that he broke the thunder with a snare, he meant that he was clumsy but very strong.

zee neenł'aanh," beeznee. Kk'ʉdaa nonee yʉgh neeneeyo. Ts'ʉh kk'ʉdaa yeneeł'aanh.

like this? Look at it anyway," the man replied. K'etetaalkkaanee went back to him and looked at it.

Ts'ʉh yʉgh neenoyeeneetonh kk'e deyeeloh. Dehoon tl'ogho yʉh yaałk'engheeluk. Ts'ʉh yʉh yenaaldluyh. Soohoonaaney.

K'etetaalkkaanee put it back in place. He wrapped a string around it very tightly and broke the tooth—on purpose, of course.

Huyeł hʉn, "Hu! Hʉgen yeł deyeeloh eehu? Neełghʉ noydaałdoh deyeełenh?" yełnee.

The man said, "Hey! It must have taken a lot of power to do that! How about using that power to fuse it back together?" the man said to him.[4]

Ts'ʉh kk'ʉdaa koon yʉh yedaatldooł dehoon neełloy noydegheeyeł. Ede degheet'aa' ts'e denoyeeloh.

Then K'etetaalkkaanee blew strongly on it and mended it. It was as if it had never been broken.

"Baasee' enaa baasee'! Daadeyetoleeł beesnee dʉhʉgh gheel go dosneehee," detaalnee'.

"Thank you, thank you very much! I knew he could do it; that is why I asked him," the man said.

Kk'ʉdaa go eet koon ło'ts'eyʉh hoozoonh ts'e tlede gheelet, go k'enaałdon' ts'en'. Ts'ʉh eet hełde nełtseeł eldlaat gheelhee. Bedełnee'aa. Nedaanh ghulaa' nełtseeł eldlaat eehu. Go edeyʉh eeydee nelaanh ts'e haadeeyo *or* doogh zo eeydee eenh go eet hełde

Then K'etetaalkkaanee spent a good night with them and filled himself with food. The man must have become a wolverine, but the story does not say that. I don't know when he became a wolverine. All the others had always become animals and left, but it

4. When K'etetaalkkaanee broke the tooth, he was showing off. The wolverine man knew K'etetaalkkaanee had done it with medicine power.

ghulaa'. Ts'ʉh neɫtseeɫ zaa'en nelaanh. Ts'ʉh kk'ʉdaa go eeydee
kkaa koon ghʉ haanodeedeyo.

does not say that here. He was a wolverine, though. Then K'etetaalkkaanee left once again.

Behookkaay Denaa
Shovel Man

Ts'ʉh yoogh koon kk'ʉdaa ghehoł, ghehoł, ghehoł. Huyeł hʉn doogh hʉn denaa kk'e hoolaanh. Ts'ʉh ehu ghehoł. Doogh hʉn ten gheelhee. Do'o hʉn yeh hoolaanh. Ts'ʉh gheel eet koon kk'ʉdaa hedoneeyo. Huyeł doogh hʉn yeh denaa kkelaa. Doogh yeh ledo. Donłe neełts'e henohaak'eghede-taaldlo.

Again, he walked and walked and walked. He came upon someone's tracks and he followed them. He was walking on a path. He came to a house and went inside. No one was home. He stayed in the house. He stoked the fire and got it going again.

Eet ledo. Huyeł hʉn nots'ot'ustl eetl'ekk. Hełts'en' hʉyeł hʉdegaał nots'eel'ots eetl'ekk. Huyeł dodʉlt-ts'e hʉn haał leł hʉy ghelts'ok. Ts'ʉh yoolneek. Dehoon gheel yeneeł'eelaa. Go denaa neeł'eelaa.

He was sitting in the house when he heard someone coming home. It was evening when he finally heard someone come home. Someone handed a backpack down through the smoke hole, so he took it. He could not see the other person. He did not see the man.

Ggʉh gheelhee, gen eehu, go hʉn baabe beyeet. Ts'ʉh eeydee gheel nonł enodetaadleneek. De-hoon dodʉggʉ kkʉno hʉtleekk'e dots'el'ots go haał leł hʉy ts'egheełtonh denh, hʉts'e hʉn:

In the pack were some rabbits or some other kind of food. He started to cook them for himself. The man up on the roof began to sing after he handed down the backpack:

"Debaa sekkʉnkk'aa neeyo hee? Debaa sekkʉnkk'aa neeyo hee?"

"Who came in my absence? Who came in my absence?"

Tlaa hedodetoneyhdlee. Kk'ʉdaa k'enodaadleneek. K'egheehon'. Dodʉggʉ huts'e, "Debaa sekkʉnkk'aa neeyo hee? Debaa sekkʉnkk'aa neeyo hee?" Kk'ʉdaa hʉn koon hełts'edogho dohʉdaaneełneek. Kk'ʉdaa hʉn koon tlede dohʉdołneyhtl. Dehoon gheel nelgedee ts'ʉh gheel tlee'eełoyaa gheelhee. Huyeł gheel kk'ʉdaa hʉn yʉh beł ooteneeldaah eehu.

The man never stopped singing. K'etetaalkkaanee cooked for himself and ate. That man was still singing "Who came in my absence? Who came in my absence?" The entire evening passed and he was still up there. He stayed up there singing in the middle of the night. Maybe K'etetaalkkaanee was afraid, because he never went outside. He went to bed and tried in vain to go to sleep.

Ts'ʉh, "Hʉdee---yh! Deyeh hedonotodoł ts'e haahaa dont'aay dodʉggʉ dedaadeyogh? Doogh ees neyeh hoolaanh," nee.

Finally, K'etetaalkkaanee said, "Hey! What's the matter with him? Can't he even enter his own house? This is your own house!" K'etetaalkkaanee said gruffly.

Hedodegheetset. Dehoot'aa. No'o doyegge hʉts'e nok'olgok eetl'ekk.

The man stopped singing. It was quiet. Then he heard something slide off the roof.

Degheel kk'ʉdaa yʉh beł eenaadledaakk. Go beł ede needozaaneełtaanh ts'ʉh. Kk'ʉdaa yoogh kk'ʉdaa koon tlede beł k'enoltenh gheelhee. Ts'e koon kk'ʉdaa ts'aaneelet. "Haa! Hot'aanh denh," yeneelenh. Ts'ʉh gheel degge daats'eneełneek. Donts'e zo tl'ee go bek'ek'el ledlo.

K'etetaalkkaanee must have fallen asleep after that. He had not slept until then. He slept the whole night through. Then he woke up and thought, "Oh yes! I remember." He got up. The man's bedding was still rolled up across the room, unused.

Ts'ʉh gheel naa'en tleetaalyo. Do'o hʉts'e go nots'olgok eetl'ekk

K'etetaalkkaanee went outside and went over to the place where

t'aanh denh. Do'o hʉn koon behookkaay haanaaneetonh. Behookkaay naaghelgok łonh. At'eeyło behookkaay denaa. O ts'ʉh kk'ʉdaa hedonots'eet'ots. Ts'ʉh koon nok'ets'odon' gheelhee. Ts'ʉh eet koon kk'ʉdaa haanozeet'ots.

he had heard something slide off the roof. Lying against the wall was a wooden shovel. The shovel had slid off the roof. Apparently that man had been a shovel man. K'etetaalkkaanee went back inside and ate one more time. Then, once again, he left.

K'etleedzode

Hawk Owl

Ts'ʉh kk'ʉdaa yoogh ghehoł, ghehoł, ghehoł. Kk'ʉdaa koon yoogh nedaats'e neenok'odoł. Hu gheel kk'ʉdaa go hʉn sołt'aanh yaan' saakkaay yeł ledo de koon kk'ʉdaa neeyo. Go ede det'aanh ts'e łaałdoy neeneeyo de dekkaa' dełgheł. Ts'ʉh kk'ʉdaa hedoneeyo.

Huyeł go hʉnde sołt'aanh yaan' yeh ledo denh. Bedenaa' kkaa koonh tohne beyeł yeh daadletl'ee. "Go ło do'eent'aa?" beeznee go sołt'aanh.

"O mendon t'aanh hebeto' hebʉgh en notaałeyo," yełnee. "Nonaan nooyee t'aanh en notaa-łeyo," nee.

"O! Oho'," yełnee.

Ts'e doogh o yek'egheełon' gheelhee. Ts'e doogh hedaadletl'ee. Huyeł hʉn yoogh tleenoggʉyhhel-deyhtl, go saakkaaye. Huyeł hʉnde k'eełekk'enh hʉn hedono'eeltluh.

"Eenaa, nonaan nooyee hʉts'e eetaa' ezeł eetl'ekk!" nee.

He walked and walked and walked. He walked for a long time. He came upon a place where a woman was living with her children. As usual, he went up to the entryway, brushed off his feet, and went inside.

He saw that the woman was home. Three children were home with her. He asked the woman, "How are you? Why are you home alone?"

"Oh, this morning their father went hunting. He went hunting again," she told him. "He went hunting in the woods across there," she said.

"Oh, okay," he replied.

Then she fed him. They were sitting around. The children kept running outside. Suddenly, one of the children rushed back inside.

"Mom, we heard dad yelling in the woods across there!" the child said.

"Dodnee ts'en'?" yełnee.

"What was he saying?" she asked him.

"'Nooyee nosek'edetaałegges!' nee eetl'ekk."

"We heard him say, 'Something is dragging me into the woods!'"

Naa'en tleehʉhʉnaaneełyoot gheelhee. K'ehoolaatltl'onh. Huyeł hʉnde, "Degonaa'! Degonaa'! Dego nooyee nosek'edetaałegges!" ts'ednee eetl'ekk, bekkun' hʉn nee eetl'ekk.

Everyone rushed outside and listened. She heard her husband say, "Help! Help! Something is dragging me into the woods!"

Ts'ʉh gheel, "Benodeeneeyh! Benodeeneeyh!" nee ts'e taalzeeł. Ło'ts'eyʉh go doghunaah gheelhee dehoon gheel bendohdeełyonee dont'aa ghulaa'. Go yʉh nee'oo-naaneełneeyaa koonh. Kk'ʉdaa t'aanh.

She started shouting, "Let it go! Let it go!" In the meantime, I guess, K'etetaalkkaanee just observed what was happening. He did not even try to help. Then they heard nothing more.

Huyeł hʉn, "Sednaa', yʉhto' kk'aa ʉhdaał. Go ees tl'ok," hʉł-nee. Go nedaanh k'edee kk'ʉdaa neek'edaaneelet. Ts'e go tl'ok hʉtʉgh etldaatl. O go k'etlekk'aa. Nonaan t'aanh. Ts'ʉh hedeto' kk'e hodeł. Huyeł doogh hʉn lekkone. Ts'ʉh heyegheehon'.

After a while, she said to the children, "My children, go after your dad. Here's a dish." How presumptuous of her! What if he had not caught anything? She gave each of them a dish. Well, I guess they were hungry. They all went across a river or lake and into the woods. They followed their father They saw some blood on the trail and ate it.

Ts'e yoogh dehoot'aa. Dednaa' kkaa yeł no'eedeyo. Huyeł hʉn

Some time passed. The man came home with his children. His

ło'ts'eyʉh denaaggaade aalekkondeelenh. Ts'ʉh neets'enaaneek'eł łonh ts'e gheel nots'eet'ots. Dednaa' kkaa yeł no'eedeyo. K'ek'ʉh yoze no'eet'onh. At'eeyło ggʉh tl'etlt'o yeyeł honotlaatleełdegheełnenee.

forehead was bleeding. He came home with his face all scratched up. He returned with his children and brought home a little piece of fat. Apparently he had thrown an axe into the rabbit's shoulder blade, and it got stuck.

Go betl'etlt'o gheel eey go k'ek'ʉh heneetonh. Ts'ʉh eeydee yeł honotlaatleełdegheełnenh. At'eeyło ggʉh ggoken ghʉ tlaatleeł daaneełnenh. Go ye'ooneelaa' denh.

You know how there is a layer of fat between the shoulder blades. He threw the axe through its shoulder blade while hunting it. When he pulled his axe free, the fat came out on it.

Eende nobeytaałegges go detlaatleeł ootunh dehoonh. Ts'ʉh kk'ok'eyeeggaas dehoon ent'aa go, "Gonaa'!" noo. "Go nooyee nooe k'edetaałegges!" nee. Ts'ʉh be'ot yʉgh deyenee'eł'aanh ts'ʉh, "Benodeeneeyh!" yełnee. Ts'ʉh go detlaatleeł gheel hono'oonee'o'. Go yaadenh dotoneeł eenhdenh. O bedo' gheelhee hono'oonee'o'. Huyeł hʉn ggʉh tl'etlt'o hʉk'ʉh yeł honoyedegheełnenh. Ts'ʉhʉkk'aatʉgh gheel go ggʉh koon beggoken dezet. Go hʉgh tlaatleeł daalnenh denh.

The rabbit began to drag him while he held on to the axe. It was when he was being dragged around that he yelled. He yelled, "Something is dragging me back into the woods!" That's when his wife became worried and told him, "Let it go!" Then he tried to free his axe because he could not make a living without it. Maybe it was his beak.[1] When it finally came out, there was some fat on it from between the shoulder blades. That is why the rabbit has a hole on its shoulder blade to this day. It is where the axe went through.

Ts'ʉh kk'ʉdaa go k'ek'ʉh doogh gheel neets'enee'onee. Ts'e go koon ehu donaah. Ts'e go

The man put the fat down somewhere. I don't know what K'etetaalkkaanee was doing

1.In stories, a bird person's axe becomes its beak when the person is transformed into a bird.

yekk'aadeel'aatl. Huyeł bekkaa-tl'ohheyeetlt'eh, go K'etetaal-kkaanee. Nonts'e letaanh dehoon neełkk'e dokkaak'eghaaldlo.

"Heen', denaaghʉ ts'enee'ots de ho nʉgh k'ek'ʉh yeł nok'eneedlut," ts'ednee. Doogh neets'enee'onh beeznee hu yokko hoonaatl'aan'. Huyeł bekkelaa. Doogh hʉneeł'aanh eehoo.

"Ho nʉgh neens'onh denh," ts'ednee.

Huyeł go yeggenhyoze k'eełekk'ee gheel hʉn, "Eenaa, nʉgh ees neeyonenh kkaatl'oh he'etlt'eh," yełnee.

Oh my! Ts'ʉh gheel eet gheel noyoolneek, go k'ek'ʉh yozee.

"Hʉ seyeł hot'aanh... Go ło nedaats'e detl-'aanee," nee gheelhee. Go k'ek'ʉh yozee.

Ts'ʉh kk'ʉdaa nonł noyeenaaldlut. Hʉn koon yʉh deneeltots. Ʉhts'e gheel go heghe'ene nonaałdlode zoo' edetʉgh noltseeyh tʉh tl'ogho yʉh deneeltus beeznee. Nonł hʉn koon yʉh k'ʉhgaal tl'ok dʉgh denoltots gheelhee go nonaałdlode. Kk'ʉdaa eeydee naa'etltseenh.

around there, but he stepped on the fat, and it stuck to the bottom of his foot. He went across the room and lay down with his legs crossed.

The man said, "Honey, we have a visitor. Why don't you make some ice cream with that fat?" She began to look for the fat where he said he had put it. It was gone. She looked for it in vain.

"I put it right there," the man said.

Then one of the children said, "Mom! It's stuck to the bottom of the visitor's foot."

Oh my! She must have taken back that little bit of fat.

K'etetaalkkaanee said, "Ah, I'm just not myself. How could I have done that?" There was just a little piece of fat.

The woman began to make ice cream with it. Soon it rose and became large. That is why Indian ice cream increases in volume if it is made correctly. The ice cream became so big that it almost rose above the sides of the pan. She made it.

Dehoon hʉn saakkaay hʉn aanhʉdaadlenenh. Yʉh heldlo. Haabaanhʉdaadlenenh.

Meanwhile, the children had all become ill. They were lying around, sick. All of them were ill.

"Nʉgh ees nedenaa' kkaa aanhʉdaadlenenh," nee gheelhee go sołt'aanh.

"Your children have become sick," the woman said.

Ts'ʉh, "Yeey! Daahedeyoh ts'en'?"

He said, "Oh my! What happened to them?"

"Ghulaaa'!" "Doht'aa?" hebeez-nee.

"I don't know!" "How do you feel?" she asked them.

Huyeł, "O yʉh yenk'ets'enee-don' kk'e dehoot'aa," hednee gheelhee.

"We feel as if we have eaten too much, they replied."

Ts'o ghool go ghulaa', "Genee ohhon'?" hebaanh hebełnee.

Their mother asked them, "What did you eat?"

Huyeł, "K'ełekk'aatlene' ts'egheehon'," hednee. Go hełde k'ełekk'aat.

"We ate the blood of the game that had been caught," they answered. It was at the kill site.

Ts'ʉhʉ, "Yeey'! Enaa sedenaa' kkaa, ho nonaan hʉkk'e ggaasek'e-ghedeetenghee'ok hu kk'ohełedaatl denh," hʉłnee. Belkkon heghee-hon' ts'e hʉkk'aa'eelneek. Ts'ʉh kk'ʉdaa, "Heen', ho no'o beyeł-naalsyon hebʉgh hedononeelyaa haa'. Tlaa zeet," ts'ednee.

The man said, "Oh! my dear children, they went across where I was dragged and my forehead was scraped." He realized that they had eaten his blood. "Honey, go outside and bring in the thing with which I have been raised, even though it may be to no avail," the man said.[2]

2. The phrase "the thing with which I was raised" refers to some mice feet he inherited, probably from his father.

Kk'ʉdaa naa'en t'aanh go sołt'aanh tleetaalyo. Ts'e yoogh dehoot'aa. Huyeł hʉn do'ots'e deeltsaa' kkaa' nełenłekel ggun nełełekel hʉn hedonots'eelyo. Ts'ʉh go dekkun' tl'oyegheelo. K'eełekk'e heelaanh ts'e yeggedenh koonh tl'etlt'o heyłdetl. O yoogh eey dehoon gheel dohʉdnee ghulaa'.

Ts'e yoogh ode dehoot'aa. Huyeł yennoheetaałekkooyh. Yennoheedekkuyh. Huyeł hʉn doheełt'aa'aa. At'eeyło hedeto' lekkon eenee' hegheehon aahaa hebaanhʉdaadlenenh.

Ts'ʉh kk'ʉdaa eet tlede hʉgheelet. Kk'ʉdaa go saakkaay doheełt'aa'e ts'e denaahedeyoh. O ts'ʉh gheel k'enhetllaadee. Eet hełde koon ʉhts'e beyeł ts'eseneegaa. Go k'etleedzodze beeznee ts'e hʉyaan' beyeł eseneyh. O ts'ʉh gheel k'enhetllaadee.

The woman went outside. Some time passed. Then she came back in carrying some dried mice feet that were tied together.[3] She gave them to her husband. He hit each child on the back of the neck with them. He probably said something at the same time.

Some time passed. Then the children started to vomit. They all vomited. Then they were better. Apparently they had become sick by mistakenly eating their father's blood.

The children became well and the night passed. Then they must have all been transformed, but I don't know. The story is called the hawk owl story, so they must have been transformed.

3. The mice feet have medicine power.

Delo' Ghʉ Nołedoyee

The One Married to His Own Hand

Go koon tl'ee hełde heghe'en ggołtl'oyooze ts'edetaalnee ts'en'. Go yeggenhyoze et'eghł behoolaan, kkaa saakkaay yoze hednee tʉh ggołtl'oyooze.

Yoogh ghehoł, ghehoł, ghehoł. Huyeł kk'ʉdaa yoogh koon hʉdaalkk'un' de neeyo. Ts'ʉh hedoneeyo. Huyeł go hʉn denaa ledo. Dehoon ggołtl'oyooze kkaa yeh hʉts'e aa'eelneek. Go et'eeyło bedenaa' kkaa. Go ggʉh kaadzode gheel go ggʉh lił tl'oyooze. Ho yoogh beghotleets'ełk'eyhtl te gheel eey bekaadzode bets'e le'on haał baabe laaghe. Hełde koon yoogh dekenh aaheyooghenełteeyh. Go hełde kaaghozen koonh go eeydee k'edeeteeye' yeyeł ootołolaa. Sooge koonh. Heydegheenee' de heghe'en heyeyeł haał gheeł'o'.

Eeydee kkaa yeggenhyoze kkaa hʉnde yʉh yeh hʉts'e aa'eelneek. Ts'ʉh kk'ʉdaa go beggenaa' k'enaa'etlneek. Ts'ʉh kk'ʉdaa

This is a story about why we call a newborn baby *ggołtl'oyooze.* Whenever a new baby is born, they call it *"Ggołtl'oyooze."*[1]

He walked and walked and walked. Then he came upon a place where there was fire, another home. He went inside. A man was living there. There were a lot of babies in the house. Evidently they were his children. The stubby tail of the rabbit is called *ggʉh lił tl'o yooze*. When we skin a rabbit, we usually leave the fur on the tail, using it for trap bait. The tail and fur are twisted around a stick and frozen. Small game animals like it, especially weasels, and martens too. This is what they used to say. They used to use it for trap bait.

There were a lot of these children in the house. His friend cooked. Then he began to eat. Then he served food to all of the rabbit

1. *Ggołtl'oyooze* is apparently a contraction of the words *ggʉh lił tl'o yooze*, meaning "little rabbit-skin, little buttocks, " perhaps because rabbit skin was occasionally used as baby diapers.

k'etaalhon'. Huyeł go ggołtl'o-yooze kkaa te k'etaatlkoot. Ts'ʉh kk'ʉdaa nonł dehoon edeyeł naa-hedaayh kk'aadnee. Yʉh de'ot yeł henaayh kk'aadnee. At'eeyło genee go Delo' Ghʉ Nołedoyee beeznee.

tails. While doing this, he was talking—to himself, it seemed. He sounded like somebody talking to his wife. I don't know what he was, but he is called "The One Married to His Own Hand."

Kk'ʉdaa yoogh go k'egheehon'. Ts'ʉh naaltaanh. Huyeł nonts'e hʉts'e sołt'aanh yeł henaayh kk'aadnee. Huyeł hʉn sołt'aanh aak'ehooneełlet kk'e dehʉdnee. Ts'ʉh doogh nohʉnle'eeyh gheel-hee. Huyeł denaagheneede kk'aant'aay nonts'e hʉn koon den-loggeze hʉts'enh hʉn ggʉh leł tl'oyooze yeł gheneyhtl. At'eeyło k'enohootaałdlaan'. At'eeyło delo' ghʉ nołedo. Ts'ʉh hʉn koon yʉh ggołtl'oyooze taalkk'oyh. At'eeyło k'ehoolaanh.

K'etetaalkkaanee ate and went to bed. He could hear the man across the room talking, as if to a woman. Then he heard what sounded like a woman in labor, so he peeked over at him now and then. Then, like the devil,[2] across the room the man was pulling something that looked like a rabbit tail from between his fingers. A birth was taking place. Evidently this man was married to his own hand. Soon a newborn *ggołtl'oyooze* began to cry very loudly. It had been born.

Ts'ʉh eet kk'odon koon kk'ʉ-daa ts'aaneelet. Ts'ʉh beggenaa' yenok'egheełon'. Dehoon ło'ts'e-yʉh ggołtl'oyooz kkaa yʉh yeh hʉts'e aa'eelneek. Ts'ʉh eet koon kk'ʉdaa haanodeedeyo. Yełnee ts'e hʉyaan' koon kk'ʉdaa yʉgh nohol-nek go Grandpa gheelaa'ee.

K'etetaalkkaanee woke up the next morning and his friend fed him. Many *ggołtl'oyooze* were in the house. Then he left. That was as much as my Grandpa used to say about it.

2. The Koyukon word *denaagheneede* is translated here as "like the devil." It is a mild curse and refers to a being who takes people's lives.

Neełkk'aa Oyht'aan

The One With Snowshoes Bent up on Both Ends

Go kk'ʉdaa hʉydo k'egheeyo. Kk'ʉdaa hʉn sonot dzaan nodeellot. Kk'ʉdaa hʉn dzaanh dzaaneets daa'en nohʉlgheeyh. Tledaał te nohʉdeteeyh. Ts'ʉh kk'odehun' te tleehʉloo kkokk'e ghehoł.

Dzaaneets daa'en koon kk'ʉdaa noholghaanh dehoon noozaah notluhtl, oyh yeet. Huyeł hʉn doogh hʉn ts'enee'ots łonh. Ts'ʉh yekk'e hʉneeł'aanh. Doogh hʉnde denaakk'e hoolaanh oyh yee. Huyeł hʉn nodaato'oto'e ghulaa'.

Neełkk'aats'e yʉh eenaadleyo go oyh ts'ʉhkk'e dent'aa. At'eeyło ło koon Neełkk'aa Oyht'aan. Neełkk'aats'e oyh eenaadleley yee kk'o'eedoyenh. Yoogh ʉdeek'e en kk'o'eedoyh gheelhee. Huyeł hʉn yaats'ets'e koon neenaa'edoyh. Eenh nedeenh, yaats'ets'e koonh. Go bekk'e taaghsoł yełnee dehʉgh gheelhee. Go yekk'e hehootlyokk. Kk'ʉdaa yaats'ets'e koon neenaa'edoyh. Ts'ʉh ʉhts'ts'e koon

He had been walking all winter. It was early in the spring and the days were long. The snow was thawing in the afternoons and freezing at night. He was able to walk on the crust in the mornings.

It was in the afternoon, and he was walking through the wet snow in snowshoes. He came upon a place where someone had been. He looked at the tracks. They were snowshoe tracks, but he could not figure out which way the man had gone.

It looked as if the snowshoes were bent up at both ends. The person who made the tracks is called *Neełkk'aa Oyht'aan*.[1] The tracks had been left by a person who had been walking around in snowshoes like that. He must have been out hunting. K'etetaalkkaanee followed the tracks one way and then turned around and followed them the other way. He tried to decide which

---

1. The One with Snowshoes Bent Up on Both Ends.

huneeł'aanh. Ts'uh go doyuggu ten huyaan' huneeł'aanh.

way to go to follow the tracks. He could not figure it out. He followed the tracks back and forth and looked at them. He was looking at the tracks and nothing else.

Dehoon "Hu! Nedaats'e hugh sekk'e hughok'eneedlooh?" bezaadeyoh.

Suddenly, someone shouted at him, "Hey! Why are you laughing at my tracks?"

Ts'uh neek'otleedaalnenh. Huyeł go hun koon bugh neets'o-'ustl. Huyeł hunde, "Haa! Hu k'egheetaaghsdlukk zo ło koonh. Kk'udaa yuh seholleł denh baabe kk'aat," nee.

K'etetaalkkaanee looked up. Someone was walking toward him. "Oh my! How can I laugh at anybody? I'm walking along, starving for want of food," K'etetaalkkaanee replied.

"Hmh! O tlaa eey dedeenee ts'e hogho yegge no'ots'e nonseyo hu daa'en sekk'e teehoyh. Yegge daa'en t'aas kk'olseyo hu yooyee ghesetseetl," yełnee. "Ts'uh yegge eet do'ots'e yegge dodeggets'e t'aas koon kk'olseyo. Ahu koon yooyee ghesetseetl," nee.

"Hmh! If what you say is true, follow my tracks back to where I came from. You'll come to a place where I had diarrhea," the man told him. "Then go past that place and keep following my track where I went up on the hill. I also had diarrhea up there," the man said.

"O! Oho', ggenaa', enaa baasee'," nee dehoon naa'en gheel yedeełgho taalyo. "Nedaats'e soo' dehełnee?" yoodnee. Ts'uh go dotlents'e kk'oleyo łonh hu dotlen taalyo. Huyeł hunde huy k'eldo de nelyo łonh. Ts'uh eeydee gheel laatlghaanh. Ts'uh kk'udaa yoogh

"Oh okay, friend. Thank you very much," K'etetaalkkaanee replied, and he started off in the direction the man had told him to go.[2] K'etetaalkkaanee was thinking, "I wonder what he meant by that." He walked down to where the man supposedly first had

2. The way the man talked let K'etetaalkkaanee know that he was being directed to something important.

yʉgh kk'ołeneek. Ts'ʉh kk'ʉdaa naa'en daa'en koon tl'ee go degge-ts'e koon kk'olseyo nee ts'ʉh.

Huyeł go hʉn koon bedzeyh dodaaltaanh. Eeyet koon kk'ʉdaa hʉyee ts'aahoonee'onh. Ts'ʉh go kk'ʉdaa go nelaan nekogh et'aanh. Ts'ʉh doogh hen hokko kk'ʉdaa hoonaatl-'aan'. Teey eełodaa de hʉn hen hoolaanh. Ts'ʉh doogh tl'odon nen' deggehu dent'aa hu gheel kk'ʉdaa neenok'etaałeghaak. Neenok'edeghaayh. K'ʉdaa baabe eet neeneelo. Go nelaan hʉlookk'ʉdogho he'elen.

diarrhea. There he came upon something in its den.[3] He killed and butchered it and started off again to where the man had told him to go.

He came to a place where the man had killed many caribou. K'etetaalkkaanee butchered all of the caribou. He had a lot of meat. He began to look around for a river. He came upon a river not too far from there. He began to carry the meat to a place on the riverbank where the ground was high. He kept carrying the meat there until he had brought all of the food. He had enough meat to last all spring.

3. He came upon a bear. Large game animals are treated circumspectly, their names seldom mentioned outright.

Ts'eyee Gheeyo Denh
Where He Spent the Spring

Ts'ʉh go tl'otne tlenen' nee'oy tleekk'e kk'ʉdaa neenok'odeghaak. Kk'ʉdaa eet ts'eyee taalyo. Dehoon hʉlookk'ʉdogho ode kk'oyenee'ee-deleet, "Go ło nedaats'e hełde kk'ʉ-daa haahaa hen dodo' detaaghs-neeł?" yeneelenh. Go needzets'e hʉyaan' hek'ehoodenee ts'ʉh, "Needze taaghskkaał," yeneelenh. Yoogh k'ededelaayh koonh.

Ts'ʉh kk'ʉdaa deyh koon no-daadlet'aa gheelhee. Ts'ʉh eeydee gheel neeł'aanh. Huyeł go yeyaa-dle yʉgh hʉgheehon neeł'aanh. Go beedoy yełts'edneegaa eenh ʉhden-t'aay taaghetltseeł yeneelenh. Huyeł hʉn, "Go neełkk'aats'e ee-naadleyo daa' hełde... Yoogh ne-daats'e detaaghsleel yee needze taaghskkaał," yeneelenh. Deyh yaadle hełde tl'ogho yʉh k'etlaat kk'aant'aa gheelhee. Go beyee koon hoolaanh. Ts'ʉh kk'ʉdaa eey-dee needaaneeł'aanh.

Ts'e yoogh ledo. Dehoon kk'ʉ-daa gheel tohʉdeleet. Kk'ʉdaa hʉn łoo koon ooldaakk. Ts'ʉh go, "Tlaa eey gen soo' tototeeł?" yeneelenh. Ts'ʉh kk'ʉdaa go dekenh leł

He carried all the meat to the high ground along the riverbank. He spent the spring at that place, but all spring he thought, "How am I going to go downriver from here?" It is easier to go downriver than upriver. "I will go down-river," he thought. He killed some game now and then.

One day, he cooked himself a spruce grouse. He looked at it. He looked at the breastbone after he had eaten the meat. He did not know about canoes, but he decided to make one. "I will make one somehow and go downriver in it," he thought. "Well, maybe if I bend up each end..." Spruce grouse breastbones are shaped like the bowpieces of a canoe. They are hollow too. He decided to use it as a model.

He stayed there. The ice was breaking up. The river was clear of ice. He thought, "I wonder what kind of bark will float." Then he looked at the bark of

ekk'oyeneek'eełleet. Ts'ʉhʉ ts'ebaa lotlaakk haadeneełkooł. Ts'ʉh kk'ʉdaa eeydee toghee'ʉh dehoon yoonługh nohʉdaałdonh de yengge toteł gheeyo. Ts'ʉh eet ledo.

different trees. He peeled off some spruce bark. He put it into the water and it started to float downstream around the bend. He ran across a short portage. He waited.

Huyeł doogh hʉn yʉh go taadeeghelggʉstl. Toyołteelaa. "Tl'ogho eeydee ees nedeenh," yeneelenh.

The spruce bark floated downstream, submerged. It did not float on the surface, so he thought, "No, I can't use that."

Ts'ʉh kk'ʉdaa t'egheł leł koon kk'ʉdaa denloh. Ts'ʉh eeydee koon toghee'ʉh. Ts'ʉh kk'ʉdaa eeydee negge koon toteł naaghedeyo. Ts'ʉh yoodo dots'en ledo. Huyeł hʉdegaał donługh hʉndenh. Beyee nodegheełtseł. Ts'ʉh taadaaneeł'onh. Dchoon gheel o toyoteeł eenhde edetʉgh yʉh toyołteelaa.

After that, he tried the bark of a cottonwood tree. He threw it into the water. He went over the portage again and waited for it there. Finally it floated out. It was soaked through and submerged. It floated, but it was still not right.

Ts'ʉh kk'ʉdaa yoogh ode ledo. Ts'ʉh kk'ʉdaa kk'eeyh leł koon kk'ʉdaa togheełkooł. Eeydee negge koon kk'ʉdaa toteł naaghedeyo. Ts'e yoogh eet ledo. Eeyet ledo. Huyeł hʉdegaał doogh hʉnde needze toyokkoł. Todokk'e toyołkełtl.

After he had stayed in camp for a while, he peeled off some birch bark. He put it into the water and went over the portage again and waited. He sat there. Finally, it floated out from around the bend. It was on the surface of the water and had no water in it. It floated on the surface of the water.

"Haa! Oho'," yeneelenh. "Kk'ʉdaa gon ees ghulaa' t'o deetaaghtlht'aa'," yeneelenh. Ts'ʉh kk'ʉdaa koon nonoo' go ts'eekkaayeh ledo de hʉts'e koon kk'ʉdaa notaałeyo.

"Ha! yes!" he thought. "This is what I am going to use." He started to walk back to the camp where he had been staying.

Kk'ʉdaa yoogh neełts'eghʉnk'edełt'es koonh. Huyeł go kk'eeyh koon deedoł. Ts'ʉh kk'ʉdaa ts'ebaa kk'ʉdaa beedoy denh laaghe denaaltleł. Ts'ʉh neełts'eghʉnyedaatlkkotl. Kk'ʉdaa beedoy denh degheeghon'. Ts'ʉh kk'ʉdaa beedoy denh daatlggunh. Ts'ʉh kk'ʉdaa yeghuts koon detaalghon'. Yeghuts degheeghon'. Kk'ʉdaa k'eenteł koonh. K'eenteł koon degheeghon'. Ts'ʉh kk'ʉdaa nełaayedeetaaldlo. Kk'ʉdaa go k'etlaat k'etlaat koon degheeghon'. Kk'ʉdaa go ede deył'aanee deyh yaadle gheel nonel'eeyh. Yekk'oyeneek'eełleet. "Gon neełkk'aats'e letonh daa' hełde eeydee t'o daadetot'aa'," yoodnoo ghoolhoo. Go yoogh ts'ebaa łaanh deelaan deełggunaayee. O go k'eggaadle ts'enh koon k'ehegheeghon'. Dehoon łaanh yoogh ede hʉnee'oodaalee'oy koon yegge yooyeh hoggetlheye'oyh. Eet hełde hoozoonhts'e heyen'ełneyh. Go łaanh deelaanh ts'ʉh, deełggunaa ts'ʉh.

He had also been splitting logs into boards. The birch had been too heavy. Then he had cut down a spruce tree for the canoe frame. He split it and made it into pieces for the frame of the canoe. He dried the boards for the frame and began to make the ribs. He made the ribs and then the crosspieces too. He made the crosspiece to go across the top. Then he began to put it all together. He had made the bowpieces too. He used the breastbone of the spruce grouse as a model. He shaped the bowpiece. "Each end will have a bowpiece," he thought. He had used some green spruce that had not yet dried. They also used to make bowpieces from big roots among driftwood. They would take the big roots from a standing tree while the roots were still green. That way the roots would be easier to carve because they would be green and not dried.

Eeydee gheel kk'ʉdaa yeghenee denloh. Ts'ʉh neełkk'aats'e k'etlaat yʉgh needaaneelo.

He prepared the needed materials to make the canoe. Then he put the two bowpieces on either end.

Yoogh ts'aa netoogh hee. Go hʉlookk'e dogho daaneełlot ts'ʉh. Go nelaan et'aanh eeydee kkaa ledo. Kk'ʉdaa eeydee gheel aayedaaneelo. Ts'ʉh kk'ʉdaa yeyee

This whole process probably took him a long time because it was a long spring. He was living on the meat that he had. He attached the frame to the bowpiece. Then he put

k'eghuts degheelo. Kk'ʉdaa k'eentel koon nʉ'ʉndaaltleyh. Kk'ʉdaa eey dehoon gheel dek'etolk'eł ts'e dehoodeyoghee. Go kk'ʉdaa dek'eedletsegaa ts'ʉh.

in the ribs, and then he put on the top crosspieces. It was the time of year when the trees could be easily peeled, when the sap was not dried up.

Kk'ʉdaa kk'eeyh detaatl-'aan'. Kk'eeyh lel degheeł'aan'. Kk'ʉdaa eeydee yʉgh neeneelo. Go hʉyh koon negheełk'eł. Ts'ʉh kk'ʉdaa eet kk'ʉdaa yʉh baahaa kk'oyedetolkkon yeł yeghenee neek'eneelo. Ts'ʉh go yʉgh kk'o'eedeneeyh. Kk'ʉdaa yeghenee neehooneelo.

Then he began to collect the birch. He gathered the birch bark. Then he piled it next to the frame. He also gathered some roots. He got everything ready so he could sew the birch bark to the frame. He worked on it and got it all ready.

Dehoon gheel yoogh koon yeekk'e nonohʉtaałelet. Ts'ʉh gheel yoogh beł neltenh gheelhee. Do'o t'aanh yʉgh neechooneelo. Ts'uh ts'aano'eedelet. Huyeł denaagheneede! Do'o koon yʉh bebeedoy yʉh kk'odetolkkon' ts'e hʉyaan' dent'aa. Yʉh kk'eeyh baa'eelyo gheelhee.

It was late in the evening. He fell asleep after getting everything ready. Then he woke up. What the devil? To his surprise the canoe was all ready to be sewn. The birch bark had been laid against the frame.

"Haa! Go ło debaa deyeeloh?" yeneelenh.

"Hey! Who did that?" he thought.

Ts'ʉh kk'ʉdaa yoogh koon yʉgh kk'onołeneek hʉyoze. Ts'ʉh kk'ʉdaa yoogh koon dzaan nohodelet.

Then he worked on it a little more and another day went by.

Yekk'oyeneek'eełleet. "Go ło debaa? Debaa yʉgh kk'ołeneek?" yeneelenh. "Go ło tl'ogho hootl'ełts'e beł naalgetenh."

He wondered about it. "Who was it? Who worked on it?" he wondered. "I must have slept very soundly."

Kk'ʉdaa bekk'aatolneyhtl ts'e delyoh. Ts'ʉh kk'ʉdaa gheel koon yeekk'e nonohʉtaałlet. Ts'ʉh kk'ʉdaa dek'ede'aat'on ts'ede gheel ghʉ neełt'otl. Noh kk'aa hoodletseenh. Eet hokk'aa hʉneeł'aanh.

The canoe was all ready to be finished. Again, it was late at night. He took his tanned hide blanket and made a hole in it. He made himself a peephole through which he could see.

Dehoon gheel beł hok'edenletenh. Letaanh. Yeekk'e nohole---ł. Yoo'oots'e hʉts'e hʉdedeggut eetl'ekk. Dehoon k'enaadle'eenh. Kk'e dok'enaadlekooł, go ts'ede t'oh. Do'o hʉn koon sołt'en kkaa needenaadeggut. Hʉn koon heyʉgh kk'otaałeneek.

Then he pretended to sleep. He was lying there. It was late at night when he heard some noise. He was hiding. His face was covered; he was under the blanket. Many women came to the canoe and, to his surprise, they started to work on it.

Gheel kk'ʉdaa, "Haa! Yegge ło eey dek'eelogh kkaa," yeneelenh. Tl'ogho hʉneeł'aanh.

Then he thought, "Oh, so those are the ones who did that." He watched them closely.

"Netooghe! Netooghe!" neeł'ehedednee. Dehoon kk'ʉdaa kk'ok'ehedetaatlkkon'.

They whispered to each other, "Hurry up! Hurry up!" They began to sew.

Go ełkeeh doldoy laagh ło go nonł k'etlaat ts'uhu gheel kk'ohʉdełkkonee. Huyeł go beggenaa' k'eełekk'ee hʉn, "He! Ggenaa, k'edenhne oho bʉgh kk'ohoodeneeyh. Nedaadenł'aan eeydee?" yełnee.

The woman who was to become a boreal owl sewed on an area that was to be covered up. Then one of her friends said, "Friend, why are you sewing it that way when we're making it for someone else?"[1]

"Haa! Ggenaaa', ts'eedokk'eeyh yekk'e hʉlaaghe," nee gheelhee. Et'eeyło kk'ʉdaa ts'eedokk'eeyh yekk'e hʉłtseeyee.

"Oh, friend, this part is going to be covered anyway," she answered. Evidently she was creating careless sewing in hidden parts for the future.

1. Her friend was asking why she was making sloppy, big stitches.

Dehoon yegge sołt'aanh k'eełekk'enh gheel ło'ts'e betleeghonoyesnedekkʉk, soonh aahaa. Eeydee gheel eenaatl-'aan'. Eeydee yaan' neeł'aanh. Huyeł kk'ʉdaa do'o zo neeheyeeneetonh, yʉh heyenodolnekk ts'ʉh. Heyedolnekk ts'ʉh neeheyeeneetonh.

One of the women was so pretty that her face glowed with beauty. He began to look at her. He watched only her. Soon the canoe was finished, because they all had been working together. They finished it quickly.

"Netooghe, nʉgh kk'ʉdaa ts'aatoleł," neeł'enhedetaałnee'.

"Hurry, he's going to wake up soon," they told each other.

"Haa! Debaa łonek'e yegge sołt'aanh k'edeeteey nezoon deghotley seełto'eełghole," yeenaaldleen'. Kk'ʉdaa no'o hʉneeł'aanh.

He wished, "I hope that pretty girl loses her awl." He watched them.

Huyeł hʉn, "Netooghe kk'ʉdaa ts'aatoleł. Kk'ʉdaa ts'aatoleł," neeł'ehdednee. Kk'ʉdaa hʉn koon hʉghonohegheltseet. O go hedek'edeghotley yaan'.

"Hurry up! He's going to wake up! He's going to wake up!" they told each other. They picked up their things very quickly, probably just their awls.

Huyeł hʉn, "He! Ggenaa nʉgh sedeghotley nogheegheł, go doogh t'aanh," detaalnee'. Eeydee okko nʉhʉtaadleyo. Dehoon, "Netooghe!" Naa'en k'eldon' ʉhdon haanodeededaatl. Dehoon k'ʉhtl'oghʉnh ts'e needaalnenh. O go nedaanh hʉts'enh koon bekk'aatl'o nok'eetolyeł. Ts'ʉh gheel ło'ts'eyʉh go deghotley ghe'en gheel neeke'eelgheł. Nʉhʉldeł. Beł neelteelaa gheelhee. Go benhʉdeełyonh ts'ʉhʉyaan'. Degge daaneełtset. Ts'ʉh no'o yʉh yeetlyeł.

Then the girl said, "Hey, friend, my awl fell around here." She began to search for it while the others told her, "Hurry up!" Some of them had already left. She was the last one. She could not leave without it because it was not easy to replace. She refused to go without her awl. She searched for it frantically. K'etetaalkkaanee must not have slept that night, being so enchanted. He jumped up and grabbed her.

Deetaalbaah. "Gonaa'! Go sets'oolneek!" nee ts'en'. Tl'ogho yʉh kk'ʉdaa hʉn koon yʉh taalbeh.

She began to yell. "Help! Someone grabbed me!" She was barking.[2]

Ode yoogheetunh eehoo. Ło'-ts'eyʉh oolo dodeteedleleel. Kk'ʉ-daa gheel yenodegheetset. Go belo-tl'ʉgh ts'aayeeneeyo gheelhee. Naa'en t'aanh.

He held on to her for a while but she would not stop yelling. He let her go. She must have escaped from him. She ran off.

Kk'ʉdaa beedoy dzaah koon degheeł'aan'. Ts'ebaa k'edzaah degheeł'aan'. Eeydee koon kk'ʉdaa aahaa yeeldzaakk. Kk'ʉdaa tono-yeteeyh. Hʉn koon yʉh toyokkoł. "Go ees kk'ʉdaa tl'ogho needze taaghskkaał," yeneelenh. Tʉgh'oy koon etltseenh.

He gathered some pitch for the canoe. He got some spruce pitch and sealed the canoe with it. He kept putting the canoe into the water. It floated well. "Now I am ready to paddle downriver," he thought. He also made a paddle.

Dehoon go sołt'aanh eyenee-deelaanh. Yenoyeneetełłek go he-ghelneeyh dehoon. "Tlaa eey ne-daanh hʉts'enh soo' dehet'aanh?" kk'ʉdaa yeneelenh. Kk'ʉdaa nee-k'otokkaał eenhde daa'en go hʉts'e haanaahedeededaatl hu gheel taal-yo hee. Kk'ʉdaa daa'en ehu ghe-hoł. Go yʉhʉ helonh ts'ʉh doogh zo yʉh tlee'eedegges gheelhee. Dohoot'aa deheghe'en hʉnotle don hʉtetl-'eey hu. Kk'ʉdaa daa'en ghehoł, ghehoł. Huyeł do'o hʉn kk'ʉdaa onh doy hoolaanh.

He was thinking about the girl. While he was getting ready, he thought about her now and then. "I wonder where they came from," he thought. He was ready to go when he walked over toward where they had come from. He followed their trail. Because there were so many of them, their path was well worn. I don't know why he had not seen the trail before. He walked and walked. He came to the entrance of a den.

2. The *Denaakk'e* verb for the sound she made is *taalbeh*. It suggests that she was barking like a fox.

Eet hʉneeł'aanh. Go yʉh eet hʉyenotleeghedegges. Ts'ʉh go onh doy lehaanh.

He looked at it. A well-worn path went into it. He stood at the entrance to the den.

Doyehts'e hʉn tleets'eeltluh. "Sode, 'Nenh doo'?' sełnee sode," nee dehoon deldlek deldlek kk'aa t'aanh.

Soon a girl rushed out. "My older sister told me 'How about you?' my older sister," she said, while making the noise *dlek dlek*.[3]

"Naa, nʉgh node kk'e deteghee-t'aa' eenh nenot'egge nenʉhłyee ghedetlaakk," yełnee. At'eeyło tse-gheldaale.

"No, you would be as pretty as your older sister if your eyelids didn't droop," he answered her. Apparently she was a squirrel.

"Ne'ot netl'onosołtaał." Beyeenhooldlet ts'ʉh noyegge t'aanh.

She said, "We'll give you back your wife." Then she rushed back into the house, offended.

Eet lehaanh huyeł doyehts'e hʉn koon tleenots'eeltluh. Sołt'aanh yoze yoogh yʉh nedaats'e eey kusge kk'aant'aay ts'ednee ts'en'. Koon tlee'eeltluh. "Sode, 'Nenh doo'?' sełnee sode." Yeetaatlyeł dehoon noyegge t'aanh. "Ne'ot netl'onosołtaał," daadeyoh. At'eeyło kusge.

He stood there, and then another woman rushed out. She was a very small, pretty woman—you know the expression, "as pretty as a least weasel." She rushed out next. "My older sister told me, 'How about you?'" He grabbed for her but she ducked back inside. "We'll give you back your wife." Apparently she was a least weasel.

Kk'ʉdaa doogh eet lehaanh doyehts'e hʉn koon kk'ʉdaa

He continued to stand there, and then another woman came out, one

3. Her older sister, the fox, asked her to try to attract K'etetaalkkaanee's interest. The *Denaakk'e* verb *deldlek* means "to make the sound *dlek*" and suggests the noise and movement of a squirrel. Each woman who came out of the house had a different voice, which Catherine Attla imitated while she was telling the story. The squirrel spoke rapidly.

sołt'aanh nekoh huyozeyee. Yoogh ło'ts'eyuh soonh aahaa betleeghnoyesnedekkugenh. Kk'udaa tlee'eeltluh. "Sode, 'Nenh doo'?' sełnee sode," nee. Huyeł hun yetaatlyeł dehoon, "Ne'ot netl'onosołtaał." Noyegge t'aanh. Doo', yekk'aay taaltset. At'eeyło kaaghozene.

who was a little bigger than the last. She was so pretty that her face glowed with beauty. She rushed out. Speaking slower than the others, she said, "My older sister told me, 'How about you?' my older sister." He grabbed for her, but she ducked back inside. "We'll give you back your wife," she said quickly. *Doo'*, he had grabbed for her but had failed to reach her. Apparently she was a weasel.

Ts'uh kk'udaa doyehts'e hun koon sołt'aanh tleeno'eeltluh. "Sode, 'Nenh doo'?' sełnee sode." Haa! nugh...Do'eent'aa ło go eeydee edegheenee'. At'eeyło deeltsaa'e. Eeydee hełde nedaats'e ło go de'eent'aa yełnee. Eeydee ees benolgeneh. Eeydee koon naayegge t'aanh beyeenhooldlet. Ts'uh, "Ne'ot netl'onosołtaał," nee.

Then another woman came rushing out and spoke in a high, fast voice. "My older sister said, 'How about you?'" I forgot what he said to her. Apparently she was a mouse woman. I forgot that part. She also rushed back inside angrily, saying, "We'll give you back your wife."

Yoogh dehoot'aa huyeł doyehts'e hun koon tleets'o'ustl. Sołt'aanh yok'aale. "Sode, 'Nenh doo'?' sełnee sode," nee.

Some time had passed when another woman came out slowly. She looked poor. Slowly, she said, "My older sister told me, 'How about you?' my older sister."

"Nugh node kk'e detegheet'aa' eenh nugh noh k'eleek kk'e de'eent'aa," yełnee. Go noh ede neendo yełnee.

He told her, "Oh, you would be as pretty as your sister if you weren't so much like a *noh k'eleek*.[4] That was his way of telling her she was too blind.

4. *Noh k'eleek* means "eye song" and refers to boreal owls or people with poor eyesight. Athabaskans believe that boreal owls are partially blind in daylight.

"Ne'ot netl'onosołtaał," nee. Noyegge t'aanh. At'eeyło ło ełkeeh doldoye.

"We'll give you back your wife," she said slowly. Then she went back inside. Apparently she was a boreal owl.

Ts'ʉh kk'ʉdaa yoogh ledo. Huyeł doyehts'e koon tleenots'eel-tluh. "Sode, 'Nenh doo'?' sełnee sode." Sołt'aanh tlaagge kuh.

He was still there, waiting. Another one came rushing out and spoke slower and louder and more gruffly than the others. "My older sister told me, 'How about you?'" She was a big, awkward woman.

"Nʉgh node kk'e detegheet'aa' eenh nʉgh nodootlk'eełts'ehk," yełnee. At'eeyło negoodzeghe. Go hełde neelts'eyhtl neelts'eyhtl ts'e ent'aa go nodootlk'eełts'ehk yełnee. "Ne'ot netl'onosołtaał." Noyegge t'aanh.

"You would be as pretty as your older sister if you didn't keep blinking," he told her. Apparently she was a great horned owl. He had said that to her because she kept blinking her eyes. "We'll give you back your wife." She rushed back inside.

Kk'ʉdaa yoogh t'aanh detlek-ts'e---n' tleehegheedeyhtl. Dehoon ło'ts'eyʉh yoogh daadʉht'aa daa-dʉht'aa degheenee'. Kk'ʉdaa hʉn hedaahedenaałeneek. Go sołt'aanh neteekk'ee yaan' kk'aay taaltset. Yoogh et'eeyło be'ooneeley yeh, gholey yeh ts'ednee. Ło go neeyo hʉts'enh dehet'aanh. Yoogh detlek-ts'e---n'. Taahgoodze koon nedaa-ts'e ło go de'edegheenee'? Ts'e sooge koonh.

One by one, more women came out to him. He found something wrong with each one of them. None of them had pleased him except the two that he had grabbed for and missed. It was a house of birds and small animals. It was a house of fur-bearing animals.[5] They had come to him from that place. He said something to a mink too, but I have forgotten what. There was a marten too.

5. These animals are associated with riches.

Ts'ʉh kk'ʉdaa noyeh hʉts'e hʉn gheel, "Tleek'elool ghudekkoyh," ts'ednee eetl'ekk. Kk'ʉdaa, "Tleek'elool ghudekkoyh. Tleek'elool ghudekkoyh."

He heard someone inside say, "May the entrance become big. May the entrance become big. May the entrance become big."

Yenhedeetaalneek. Noyeh hʉts'e hʉdetaałeneenh. Huyeł kk'ʉdaa tleehetaaldaatl. Yʉh k'eełhoolt'aa de yʉh detlekts'e yʉh tleeheneedaatl.

They all began chanting this song. Then the ground began to shake. They all started to come out at once. They all came out at once.

Huyeł noyeh zo yʉh łaał doyegge yot'aan' ts'e dehoodeyoh. Go hełde tleek'elool ghudekkoyh eey detlekts'e k'eelhoolt'aa denh tleeheneedaatl daa' hʉdeneekoh ts'e dʉhʉtoneeł ts'e ent'aa go tleek'elool ghudekkoyh. Kk'ʉdaa tleek'elool eedekkʉyh. Kk'ʉdaa detlekts'e tleeheneedaatl. Huyeł noyeh zo yʉh hedoso'ʉstl ts'e yʉh dehoot'aa. Ts'ʉh kk'ʉdaa noyegge hedoneeyo. Huyeł donee hʉn kk'ʉdaa ts'eldo, go beghe'en dʉhʉt'aanee. Ts'ʉh kk'ʉdaa eeydee kk'el neets'enee'ots.

Suddenly, the entryway became larger. They had chanted and come outside together to make the entryway large. The entrance had become large and they all came out. The tunnel became big enough for him to enter, so he went inside. He saw her sitting back against the wall. It was the girl he had fallen in love with. He went over to her and sat beside her.

Dehoon kk'ʉdaa bek'etaadlelon'. Kk'ʉdaa hedonok'ehetaadlekek koonh. Yoogh detlekts'e---n' baabe zoo' okko tleehete'ʉs eeydee hedaanaahelkek.

They began to feed him. One by one, they went outside and brought in food. One by one, they went outside to get good food.

Huyeł deeltsaa' ło go hʉn leggun beghok'eghaałekk'ʉsge yoogh benodzen yozee bʉgh le'on hʉn

When it was the mouse's turn, she went out and brought in a dried fish skin that had been

hedono'eet'onh. "Haa! Noh K'e-leek debaabe ts'ʉgh kk'ʉdaa tl'ogho yʉh sebaabe ehonh aahaa." Go ełkeeh doldoy debaabe daadle-koode. Ʉhts'e heghe'en ent'eey koon ʉhdehednee.

chewed on; only a little bit of meat was left on it. Disgusted, she said, "Oh that Noh K'eleek. While she's saving her food she's always eating mine." The boreal owl is known for saving food. To this day, people still say that.[6]

Noh K'eleek debaabe daadle-koot dehoon sebaabe ehonh nee ts'en'.

The mouse was implying that the boreal owl was eating the mouse's food while saving her own.

"Haa! Yʉh dohoonaaney, 'edʉgh nodenaalset'eenh,' deenee," nee hʉn go ełkeeh doldoy ent'aa go Noh K'eleek. Kk'ʉdaa koon neełts'e kkenaahedetaadleghos. Ts'ʉh kk'ʉdaa gheel heyek'egheełon'.

"Huh! Why don't you just say 'I stole it from myself?'" replied the boreal owl, Noh K'eleek. They began to argue. After the argument died down, they fed him.

Dehoon, "Seyeł noteedoyh. Seyeł needze tegheekkaał dʉhʉ-ghʉnh," beeznee. Go tl'ogho ye-kk'aa dent'aa. Go nohbaay soł-t'aanh ło'ts'eyʉh nezoonh gheelhee. Ts'ʉhʉ kk'ʉdaa beyeł noyetaałeyo, go hʉts'enh det'aanh denh. Dets'ee-kkaayeh kk'ʉdaa noheet'ots. Ts'ʉh kk'ʉdaa yoogh eet nohodedo'. Ts'ʉh kk'ʉdaa gheel neek'ohetaal-kkaanh. Et'eeyło eey go beł yee-neełtaanh hu ghoneyhtl. Ts'ʉh beyeł k'eghetołneyhdlaa. Ʉdenh yaan'.

He said to the fox woman, "Come with me, come downriver with me." The fox woman was very pretty. She left with him to go toward where he had come from. They went back to his camp. They stayed there for a while. They got ready to leave. Apparently where he was going was where he had traveled before in his sleep, so nobody could travel with him. He had to travel alone.

6. Sometimes people would try to save choice morsels of food to eat later on but end up eating them anyway. When this happens, they jokingly blame it on the boreal owl, just like the mouse in this story.

Kk'ʉdaa nodo' yeyeł needze taalkkaanh. Huyeł denaagheneede! Ło'ts'eyʉh betl'eehulez deedeggoot, go nohbaaye. Yee'! Neghaa' ts'ʉh gheel denee yeetldo dehoon so ts'ʉghʉ dok'etlkooł. Dehoon notaa-łebeh go deyeh hʉkk'aa. Notaałe-beh. Kk'ʉdaa notaałetsaah dehoon yʉh neghaa'. Kk'ʉdaa gheel neeł-lot de nee'eekkaalaa dehoon gheel neeghoneekkaanh. Ts'uh yenodegheeneek.

She left with him. Then, like the devil, the fox woman became really hot and began to perspire and her body odor became quite strong.[7] Whew! The odor was so strong that he put up a shade for her where she was sitting behind him in the canoe, but the heat was too much for her and she began to cry for her house. She had begun barking again. She would not stop and her odor was very strong. He had not gone very far in the canoe when he had to land and release her.

"Haa! Yʉh denaagheneede dont'aa yʉh betl'eehulez beyeł no-deedegoode ło go dedaadeyoghee?" yełnee dehoon yenodegheetset.

"Hey! What's the matter? Is her own odor too much for her?" he said, while releasing her.

Et'eeyło baak'enee'onh huyeł yʉh neghaa'. Nonoo' toteł hʉts'e---n' ebeh ebeh ebeh eetl'ekk. Doo' kk'ʉdaa ʉhts'e haahaa kk'ʉdaa yenodegheeneek. Kk'ʉdaa needze taalkkaanh.

Apparently that is what happened when the sun hit her. He heard her going upriver, crying "beh, beh, beh "all the way. That is why he had to release her. Then he began his journey downriver.

7. Foxes have strong body odor, especially when they are hot.

Gełtl
Fishhook

Kk'ʉdaa ʉdenh yaan' ghekkaaɬ, ghekkaaɬ, nodo' needze ghekkaaɬ. Kk'ʉdaa ts'aaghekkaaɬ dehoon yoodo hʉn taageɬtlts'etl'onh. Kk'aaghe edeyeɬ notaaɬetset. Daangge yʉh neegho'eeldzeɬ. At'eghɬ detaaɬt'aan debeedoy nooyee gheegges. Taah dleton ehok'edeedletseenh. Go k'oolkkoyh kuh gheel go taah dleton beezneey hee. Taah dleton ehok'edeedletseenh. Notlen taaghelzoot.

Ts'ʉh dodo' needze ghebaaɬ. Yegeɬdle etlyeɬ. Nedaats'e ɬo yegge k'ets'eeɬgeɬtl huyeɬ honots'edentsek, honots'edentsek. Hoyedengheetset. Ło'ts'eyʉh begeɬdle yeetlyeɬ. Doo' nonoo' haano'eedebaanh taah kkaatl'ogh donoo'. Ts'ʉh kk'ʉdaa yoonee debeedoy ghʉnh denaa enoɬdlaat. Kk'ʉdaa tonoɬeyo ts'ʉh kk'ʉdaa debeedoy ghʉ, "Tl'ogho nedaanh neeyeeghuteeɬ?"

Then he paddled alone. He paddled and paddled downstream. As he came around a bend, he saw someone fishing with a fishhook at the far end of the straight stretch ahead of him. He pulled himself back around the bend and quickly paddled ashore. It was to be the first of many times that he would pull his canoe up onto the bank. He turned himself into a big pike. The big pike is called *taah dleton*[1] because it rests, motionless, under the surface. He turned himself into a big pike and slid into the water.

He swam downriver and grabbed the man's fishhook. You know how you jerk a fishing line, pulling the fish's head out of the water. This man jerked the pike's head out of the water. The pike yanked the fishhook from the line and, *doo'*, swam upstream with it deep under the water. He went back to where he had left his canoe and turned back into a person. As he went up the bank to his canoe, he wondered where he was going to put the hook.

1. "That which stays still in the water."

Hʉyeł deneyh ts'e yeyeł deneyh. Deyenh ts'e yekk'aa'eelneek. Ło'ts'e yooyegge neeyeghu'oł de hedenh. Yokko nʉhʉtolyaah ts'e hʉyeł deneyh. Yengheeł'aan'. Ts'ʉh gheel dek'ek'etlaat aak'edeneetonh. Koon nosoonhu nełaakk'aa doldoyee. Go denh k'eełekk'ee haadeneetonh. Ts'ʉh eet hʉt'ey degheetonh. Ts'ʉh dek'ek'etlaat yeyeł okk'aa nodegheetonh.

K'etetaalkkaanee had realized that the other person knew what he had done. It became apparent to K'etetaalkkaanee that this person was a medicine person. He did not have any place to hide the fishhook. He knew that the man would search for it, having seen him. He took a board from his bowpiece, which had just been made. He removed a board, put the fishhook into the groove, and put the board back over it.

Debeedoy tonogheegges. Kk'ʉdaa nodo' needze notaałekkaanh. Yʉgh neeghoneekkaanh. Donggʉ zo ts'eldo. Debeedoy dʉggʉ neeneegges. Dehoon nodegge yets'e hotaalyo.

He dragged the canoe down the bank and into the water. Then he continued to paddle downstream. He paddled to the man. The man was sitting on the bank. K'etetaalkkaanee landed and dragged his canoe onto the beach and went up the bank to him.

"Heey'! Bezaa'en tl'eegho naaghtl-'aan' oodesnee," nee gheelhee. Doogh yeneeł'aanh. Hʉyeł hʉn, "Bezo tl'ogho hodenaaghstset," yełnee.

The man said, "Yes, I thought I saw him." He looked closely at K'etetaalkkaanee. "Yes, I jerked his face out of the water," he said.

"Ggenaa, nedaats'e ghulaa' dehedeenee?" yełnee.

"Friend, I don't know what you're talking about," K'etetaalkkaanee replied.

"Nedaakoon bets'e hʉtaaghsts'eet soodeghoonee'yu. Ees nenaaghtl-'aan'. Sek'egełdle setl'ono-

"Don't think that you're going to fool me. I saw you. You have to give me back my fishhook. Friend,

teghee'oł ts'ʉhʉyaan'. Ggenaa', ees baadenh setegheełdlooh ts'ʉhʉyaan'," yełnee.

you're going to starve me if you keep it," the man told him.

"Ggenaa, gen ghulaa' dodeenee?" yełnee.

"Friend, I don't know what you're talking about," K'etetaalkkaanee replied.

"Ees nenaaghtl-'aan'," yełnee.

"I saw you," the man said.

Kk'ʉdaa bek'eyegheełon'. Dehoon kk'ʉdaa go doogh go de'aat'on tlaagge neyedaalkool kk'ʉdaa detlekts'e yekot'e detlekts'e nʉhʉtaadleyo. Kk'ʉdaa go yoogh ts'eyee ledloy yoze koon detlekts'e te nʉhʉlyaah.

Afterward the man fed him. After the meal, the man began to search him all over, through a leather parka that he was wearing and under all of his clothing. He searched through the few things that K'etetaalkkaanee had in his canoe.

"Nedeenh ggenaa', ees hʉyeł ts'eseneegaa ts'e ent'aa eey dehedeenee," yełnee.

K'etetaalkkaanee told him, "No, friend, I don't know what you're talking about."

"Ees nenaaghtl-'aan'. Ggenaa, setl'onoteghee'oł ts'ʉhʉyaan'."

"I saw you. Friend, you have to give it back to me."

Yets'e beyeenhułdledaa zaa'ene. Go nełaahenleget gheelhee. "Setl'onoteghee'oł ts'ʉhʉyaan'. Ees setegheełdlooh. Baadenh dotaaghesneelee? Ggenaa, nʉgh nets'eey nodetaaghs'ʉh ts'ʉhʉyaan'," yełnee.

The man was not angry with him. Perhaps they were afraid of each other's power. "You have to give it back to me. You're going to starve me. What will I do without it? Friend, I have to take your canoe apart," the man told him.

"Ggenaa, baadenh dotaaghsneel eey dodeeneeyee?" yedetaalnee'.

"Friend, what am I going to do without the canoe?" K'etetaalkkaanee asked him.

"Nedeenh, gonh dodo' telgheekkaale, segeɫdle yeɫ. Ees nenaaghtl-'aan'," yeɫnee.

"No, you will not go past here with my hook. I saw you."

Kk'ʉdaa nedaats'e needok'eheghedodenoɫ. Soot'e yekk'aa'eelneek kk'aadeyoh gheelhee. Ts'e go yek'ek'etlaat ekk'ohootaatl-'onh. Go beedoy denh haadeneetonh huyeɫ hʉn go hʉn hʉt'e dee'onh.

They argued back and forth for a long time. Then the man figured it out and began to take a piece from the bow of the canoe. He removed a board, and there was the fishhook.

"Bezo oodesnee. Tl'ogho naaghtl-'aan'," yeɫnee. "Anaa seggen'aa', kk'ʉdaa nodo' gheekkaaɫ," yeɫnee. "Ees kk'ʉdaa segeɫdle no'es'onh," nee.

"I knew it. I really saw him," he told K'etetaalkkaanee. "My dear friend, now you can paddle downriver," he said to him. "I have found my fishhook," he said.

Kk'ʉdaa eet o yoogh yeyeɫ tlede gheelet gheelhee. Nedaats'e ghulaa'? Kk'ʉdaa eet koon hʉgh haanodeedekkaanh.

K'etetaalkkaanee must have spent the night with him. I don't know. Then he left in the canoe once again.

Begho Kk'ʉsk'eghedeeghuł'o' Soo' Gho Kk'ʉsk'eghedee'onh

How Unlikely to be Hanging By the Neck From That

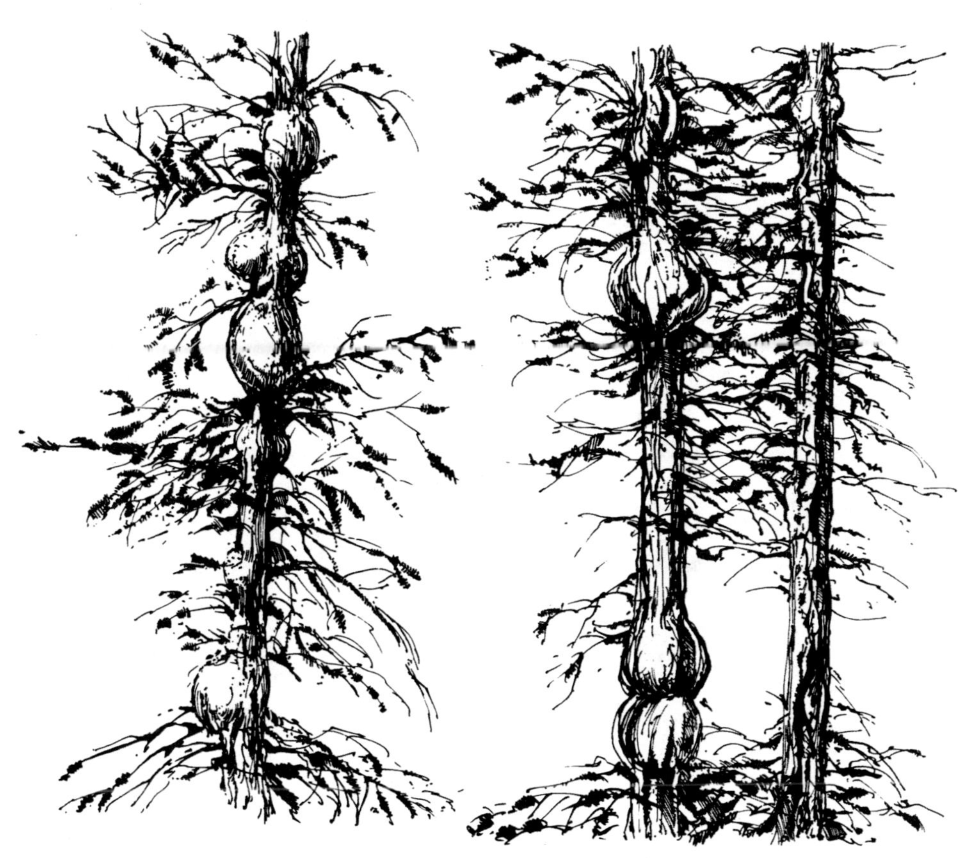

Kk'ʉdaa nodo' needze ghekkaał. Needze ghekkaał, ghekkaał. Kk'ʉdaa koon yoogh ts'aano'eede-kkaanh. Huyeł hʉn yoodo hʉts'e ts'aaneekkaanh denh yoodo hʉn nonohooltseen'. Go ede det'aanh ts'e daangge yʉh neegho'eeldzeł. Kk'ʉdaa debeedoy nooyee ghee-gges dehoon nodo' k'eenaadle'eenh. Kk'ʉdaa aado eeyet go nonohool-tseenh de neek'enaal'eenh. Daan-gge yoogh zo tonotleełegges.

Then he continued to paddle downstream. He paddled and paddled downstream. Again, he came out from around a bend. At the far end of the straight stretch, a weir had been built across the river. As usual, he quickly paddled ashore. He dragged his canoe back into the woods and began to sneak down toward the weir. He crept down to where the weir was. A well-worn path led up the bank.

Kk'ʉdaa dotlee nonohooltseen' de neeneeyo. Ts'ʉh netlaahok'enaa-dletuł. Deghokk'ʉshok'eghedee-t'onh. Taakeghaaleeyoy. Degho-kk'ʉshok'eghedeet'onh dehoon bentseyh nolekkongheele---nh. Nek'etlaahʉdelzees.

He walked up to the weir, gave himself a nosebleed, and hung himself by the neck from one of the posts of the weir—posts whose thick ends were in the water. While he hung there, his nose bled profusely. Blood flowed down from him.

Kk'ʉdaa hʉdodeggʉł eetl'ekk. Yoonuhts'e hʉts'e ts'aats'enee'ots. Dehoon go denaats'enh nolekkon-gheele---nh.

Soon he heard some footsteps. Someone came out of the woods to the bank. Meanwhile, the blood was running off him.

"Heey! Beghokk'ʉsk'eghedee-ghuł'o' soo' ghokk'ʉsk'eghedee'-onh!" kk'ʉdaa ts'ednee eetl'ekk. Go debaa yʉh soho doyeetltaanh yoodnee? Denaagheneedee kk'aan-

"Hey! What an unlikely thing to be hanging by the neck from! Didn't the man wonder who hung it up there for him?" K'etetaal-kkaanee heard him yell. "What

t'aay! Ło'ts'eyʉh saalzeeł. Bʉgh neets'enee'ots. Ts'ʉh nots'egheeł-taanh. Doogh ło'ts'eyʉh bʉk'ʉghʉ-ts'elneyh. Go zo neeneele---t. Adenk'e noteyeyee? O go neenee-let. Bets'enh nolekkongheelenh.

Kk'ʉdaa baałk'ets'engheetl'oonh. Kk'ʉdaa naangge nosaałeghaanh. Ts'ʉh go denaats'e daadebet ts'e gheel yʉh t'eyeełt'onh. Kk'ʉdaa nongge neełtʉgh nots'odeghaał. Gen nek'e yʉh ebaahoogholtsoł!

Doogh ts'etl etlyeł. Dek'etaal-hoh. Dek'ehoh dehoon ts'etl ootunh. Tl'ogho yʉh denok'enaadletl'eł dehoon hedegheetset. Yoonł ts'eenaałetek. Ts'ʉh nonee denaa-nen yʉh egguts'etltus. At'eeyło nełkkoy eyetaatltseen'.

Denaagheneede! Degge daano-ts'eneełtset dehoon t'ets'aazeelnenh. Do'o yeneeł'aanh. Ełdetl, ełdetl. Kk'ʉdaa yetaatlgus koonh eehoo. Ło'ts'eyʉh yekk'ʉghʉleneyh. Yetaatlgus. Huyeł tl'ogho yʉh ełdetl, ełdetl.

the devil!" the man began to yell excitedly. He walked over to K'etetaalkkaanee and took him down. He examined K'etetaal-kkaanee carefully. He looked dead. Wasn't he breathing? He was bleeding.

The man tied straps around the body and began to carry it back into the woods. As the man carried the body, it was facing him. He had bundled it up and put it on his back. He was carrying it back across the portage. How strong he was!

K'etetaalkkaanee grabbed a willow. K'etetaalkkaanee held onto the willow while the man jerked on him. Finally, the man gave one big jerk and K'etetaal-kkaanee let go of the willow. The man fell down hard, and as they landed, K'etetaalkkaanee dug his knee into him. Apparently he was trying to wound him.

What the devil! The man jumped back up and took off his pack. He looked at it. It jerked a little bit. He began to tickle K'etetaalkkaanee. He looked him over and began to tickle him. K'etetaalkkaanee's body jerked a little.

"Hu! Dont'aa yʉh beyee tson' k'eghaayee?" yeɫnee. Ts'ʉh kk'ʉdaa koon t'enots'eɫt'onh. Ts'ʉh kk'ʉdaa koon nongge beyeɫ haanohonhzeedeyeɫ.

"What does he think is so funny?" the man said. Once again, he put the body on his back. Bent over, he continued to carry him quickly across the portage.

Huyeɫ hʉn go ede det'aanh ts'e doogh ts'etl ɫaagheetenghʉyhdlee etlyeɫ. Kk'ʉdaa koon denok'etaadletlet. Kk'ʉdaa tl'ogho yʉh kk'aaghe neenozaat'aatl. Ts'ʉh denok'eetaadletlet dehoon yedegheetset. Yoonɫe ts'eenaaɫetek.

As before, K'etetaalkkaanee grabbed a springy willow. The man began jerking him again. The man stepped back and gave one big jerk as K'etetaalkkaanee let go. The man fell down hard.

Ts'ʉh heɫde nozeno, "Ebaa! senen!" nonee yʉh denaanen enoggu-ts'etltus neeɫk'ots'en. "He!" Kk'ʉdaa tl'ogho zeeduhu deggennohozeeltaanh. Ts'ʉh kk'ʉdaa koon yeneeɫ-'aanh. Heyedeɫnenh, heyedeɫnenh go ghetonoɫ ts'e hokko, eehoo. Dehoon eɫdetl, eɫdetl gheelhee.

Ouch! My back! K'etetaalkkaanee dug his knees into the man's back again. Ouch! That time he was barely able to get up. He looked at him again. He took the pack and hit it against the ground repeatedly to see if it would move. The body jerked a little bit.

"Hu! Beyee tson' k'eghaayee?" yeɫnee. Koonkoon kk'ʉdaa t'enots'eɫt'onh. Kk'ʉdaa naangge kk'ʉdaa beyeɫ ɫo'ts'eyʉh zeedehu kk'ʉdaa go denaanen koon kk'ʉdaa yʉh ebaa. Kk'ʉdaa dzoghoteey neenots'eedeghaanh. Nozegheeɫnenh. Saakkaay tleegguyhtlneeɫdaatl.

"Huh! What does he think is so funny?" the man said. Once again, he put him on his back. He continued to carry him back across the portage, but this time he could hardly manage to do it, his back hurt so much. He carried him back to the door of a house and threw him down. Children came running out of the house.

"Haa! Eenaa, eetaa' k'eldlaanh."

"Hey, Mom, Daddy caught something."

Noyegge hebeldon' hedonh ts'e...Ts'ʉh, "Sednaa, ho noyeh bek'etleedeenen."

Some of the children rushed back inside to their mother. The man said, "My child, go in and get the club."

Noyegge t'aanh dehoon, "Dont'aa nek'e yʉh tełdoghe," yoodnee. Yetaatldokk.

They rushed back in while K'etetaalkkaanee thought, "I hope the club disappears." He made it disappear.

"Eetaa, nedaadenh?"

"Dad, where is it?"

"Ho yehonh edʉhnee!"

"Ask your mother!"

Kk'ʉdaa hedonh koon ehednee eehoo.

They asked their mother, but she didn't know.

Dehoon no'o ts'el'onh. Doo', denaayeł nohʉdenaadlenenh.

The bundle with K'etetaalkkaanee in it was sitting outside. *Doo'*, K'etetaalkkaanee had made the man become careless.

"Ho noyeh t'aasee," nee dehoon hedonotaadletlet. Dehoon go bedenaa' kkaa koon detlekts'e yʉh yeh kk'ʉdaa hedaadletl'ee.

"It's down there in the house." he said angrily, as he rushed inside. The children were all inside the house too.

Dehoon go baahaa denaats'etlghaal dʉkk'ʉnnaatltsuł dehoon go bek'etleedeenen ts'o'oł, go yetaatldoggee. No'o łaałdoy dzoghoteey ots'enh neek'enaal'eenh.

K'etetaalkkaanee broke the straps that had bound him, and the club he had made disappear appeared in his hand. He hid outside by the door.

Noyehts'e hʉts'e, "Ho go gonh le'onh denh!" ts'ednee ts'e hʉy ts'ehʉ'oyh eetl'ekk.

He heard the man inside throwing things around, saying, "It was right here!"

Tleenohonhts'odeyełtl dehoon yetleeyee k'edegheełnenh. Ts'ʉh tleehedeyhtl ts'e detlekts'e yʉh hʉtlee' okko k'edetaatlnenh. At'eeyło koon k'eełekk'ee yoo'en ledoy, ło donggʉ nooyee ledo. Dehoon go k'ʉhdeeghʉnh. Ts'ʉh go yoo'en ledoy ts'ebaa ken t'oh ledo. Hoodletseenh de gheel ledo. Baanh bʉgh no'eełdoyaa. Baanh bʉgh nok'eedlekoodaa. Ts'ʉh gheel taaltsaah. Taaltsaah. Etseh. Kk'ʉdaa dego yʉh etseh ts'ʉhʉyʉh ʉhte gheel go yʉh denaantseyh ts'aak'eneelenh. Nek'etlaahʉloo dentseyh okko teneyh. Ts'ʉh dodʉgge ts'ebaa e'eneyh dehoon, "Yegge donłe' naahaa hʉts'e hʉtooneyh." At'eeyło koon ts'ebaa k'edzaah laaghe.

The man rushed back out, hunched over, and K'etetaalkkaanee hit him over the head. He hit all the others over the head, one by one, as they came running out. Apparently one of the girls was in puberty, so she was staying in the woods away from the house when he killed the others. This girl was staying in a lean-to under a spruce tree. The girl's mother had not come back to her for a long time. Her mother had not brought her any food,[1] so she began to cry. She began crying. She cried and cried. As she cried, her nose began to run. She wiped the mucus from her nose. She rubbed it on the spruce tree saying, "May you be something useful from now on." Evidently it was to become spruce pitch.

Go daats'e heghe'en gheel go, go yegge oonyeeyh ghʉ taak'ehetl'onh go Grandpa gheelaa' kkaa. Ʉhte hełde go Flora yeł ts'eegʉdze. O ts'ʉhʉneyh zaa'ene. "Nʉgh ts'ebaa k'edzaah oohkk'ʉsge yu. Nʉgh noghonoy ʉhhonh." Hʉy-ts'en' tʉh koonh. Taak'etlkooł. Yegge łookke noghonoy hoolaanh tʉh. "Ts'ebaa k'edzaah oohkk'ʉsk

That is why, when my grandparents had a fish trap set for blackfish, when Flora and I were little but were able to understand, they would tell us, "Don't chew spruce pitch, because you have something fresh to eat." In the fall, too, when they had a fishnet in the water, when there were fresh fish, they would tell us,

1. Girls in puberty seclusion were forbidden to eat fresh fish and game because they might bring the hunters and hunting implements bad luck. A girl's mother usually brought her specially prepared food while she was in seclusion.

yu." Go heɫde yoo'en ledoy nek'e-tlaahʉloo, go dzaah. Ts'ʉh ɫookk'e noghonoy ts'ehonh te soɫkk'ʉsgaa. Tl'ogho hʉnonɫts'e ʉhts'e hʉk'ode-naaheneeghee'enh. Yegge oon-yeeyh ghʉ taak'el'onh tʉh k'edee-teey. Dokk'o yoo'en yaats'en te gheel go teey baabe hooɫdlaa'aa. "Koyh, nedaakoon ts'ebaa k'e-dzaah oohkk'ʉsk yu," denaa'ehed-nee go heɫde go yoo'en ledoy dek'enetlaahʉloo aahaa ts'ebaa egheeneyh. Ts'ʉh yoogh ees yʉh nʉ'ʉnledlenh. At'eeyɫo baahaa ts'eeyh todedzaah dehʉgh go, "Yegge donɫe' naahaa hʉts'e hʉtooneyh," yeɫnee.

Ts'ʉh etseh. Ts'ebaa yʉh etlee-ts'eghedeneelyonh. At'eeyɫo koon ho yoogh ts'ebaa enee'on yegge ees "yoo'en ledoy tlee'." At'eeyɫo koon eeydee laaghe. Ts'ʉh kk'ʉdaa eeydee ets'eldlaat. At'eeyɫo yoo'en ledoy ote ledo dehoon go kk'ʉdaa nodo' haanodeedekkaanh. Kk'ʉdaa nodo' needze ghekkaaɫ.

"Don't chew spruce pitch." The pitch came from a girl in puberty. For that reason, we are not supposed to chew pitch when we have fresh fish. They used to watch us closely for that, especially when they had traps set for blackfish. Usually when you fish in the late winter there is not much food. "Grandchildren, do not chew the spruce pitch," they would tell us, because this girl wiped it on the tree from her nose. You can see it where it runs off the trees. It is used for sealing canoes, and this is evidently the reason that she said, "May you be useful from now on."

She cried. Soon her head grew onto the tree. Apparently her head became a spruce burl. These burls are called *"yoo'en ledoy tlee."*[2] That is what she was to be. That is what she became. While this was happening, K'etetaalkkaanee took off again downriver. He paddled and paddled downstream.

2. "The secluded one's head."

Taahgoodze Tl'en Ghʉ K'enaaneeɫtl'eɫ Denh

When He Shot an Arrow Into Mink's Leg

Needze ghekkaał, needze ghekkaał. Ts'ʉh donggʉ hʉn tso dol'onh denaa kkelaa denh. Neeghoneekkaanh. Ts'ʉh daangge totaalyo.

He paddled and paddled downstream. He came to a cache. No one was there. He paddled ashore and began to walk up the bank.

Huyeł hʉn donggʉ hʉn koon łeekkaa. At'eeyło ggaagge kuh łeekkaa bedzoten ghʉ henłekeł, go tso aahaaghedenaaneeton ghʉ neełk'ots'ene. Degedze hʉgh neełts'aagheełdaatl dehoon nodegge dodleggok. Tso yee dolyo. Huyeł go hʉn łookk'e. Go hulookk'ut te hut'aanh nedaats'e hʉk'elookk'e go, go hʉn yʉh dleghaal tso yee doldlo.

He realized that some dogs were there. The dogs were big animals and were tied to the cache posts on either side of the ladder.[1] He took his mittens and threw one to each dog, and then he ran up into the cache. He went into the cache. There were some fish. They might have been springtime fish, but there were bundles of fish there.

Go neełlot don ees go nohʉhʉlnek ts'e hʉkk'aatʉgh dleghaal hełde yendeegheegudzaa hednee. Eey go ts'eedaahaa hool'onh deheghe'ene. Dleghaal yoze Grandpa gheelaa' ees degheenee'. O go k'aalt'oodze yaan' aahaa koon k'elghaał.

They say that when people bundled fish long ago, the bundles were very small. That way they could ration the food. My late grandpa said that people used to make small bundles during hard times. The bundles were also small because they used only willow bark to bundle them.[2]

Ts'ʉh go dleghaal yoze gheel oolneek dehoon et'eeyło nodo dots'en

He took one of these small bundles. Apparently there was a

1. The "dogs" were in fact bears.

2. Willow bark is not very strong, so it could not have bound a big bundle.

tl'ee hʉtlenh ghʉ k'edaadletl'ee. Ts'ʉh kk'ʉdaa dodo' needze notaałekkaanh.

fish camp down around the bend. He began to paddle downriver.

Dodots'e hʉn koon taahgoodze noltl'ełtl. At'eeyło, "Taahgoodze, nonee tso ghʉnnondo. Nonee łee-kkaa dodnee," heyłnee, go nohʉ-tolnek heyełneeyee. Kk'odenotl'en yaakk'aa ts'aadenaaneełgheł aahaa yooneek'enh. Eekk'ok. Yedzoten ghʉ k'enaaneełtl'eł. K'ets'e nono-daadlenenh. Ts'ʉh nodo' ekk'o---yh.

A mink was running upriver on the beach. Apparently the people downriver had told her, "Mink, go upriver to the cache and see why the dogs are barking," wanting her to tell them what had happened. He took the arrowhead off an arrow and shot the shaft at the mink.[3] She screamed in pain. He had hit her in the leg. She turned around and ran downriver, screaming.

Nodo' ghekkaał. Neeghots'e-neekkaanh. Ts'ʉh go leggun ts'ool-neege eeydee gheel nosaałdon'. Nodo' hʉts'en'. Yoodo hʉts'e nee-nok'eedekk'ok. Huyeł dohʉdnee eetl'ekk.

He continued to paddle down-stream. He landed and began to eat the fish that he had taken. He could hear the mink going down-stream. She was still screaming, but then it sounded as if she had come to a stop. Then he heard people making a clamor.

"Nʉgh sołt'aanh ʉhʉdeeghee-neek," ts'ednee ts'en'.

"This woman is hurt," they were saying.

Kk'ʉdaa eet tlede taaldlet dehoon nodo hʉts'e kk'ʉdaa yen-ts'eetaałeyenh eetl'ekk. Kk'ʉdaa huyeł hʉn K'ets'eghʉltoon ło go nełe neets'enee'ots eetl'ekk.

As the night passed he heard people beginning to make medi-cine. He heard the chickadee man go to the center of the circle to make medicine.

"Sek'edzeyaa yeehulaa

Apparently the chickadee man

3. He removed the arrowhead because he did not want to kill her.

eetoon," ts'edetaalnee. "Sek'edzeyaa yeehulaa eetoon," nee eehoo.

began to sing, *"Sek'edzeyaa yeehulaa eetoon,"* he sang. *"Sek'edzeyaa yeehulaa eetoon,"* he sang in vain.

Kk'ʉdaa hʉn koon, "Nenh koonaa'," ts'ednee eetl'ekk. Neeł'enhedednee. Huyeł hʉn koon k'eden nełneeneeyo eetl'ekk.

Then K'etetaalkkaanee heard them saying to each other, "Why don't you try?" They were talking to each other. Then he heard another one go out to the center.

"Setaahooneełneek. Setaahooneełneek," ts'ednee.

"I have been pushed under water, I have been pushed under water," he sang.[4]

At'eeyło ło nołduł koon kk'ʉdaa taałeyenh.

Evidently it was the great gray owl who was making medicine.

Huyeł kk'ʉdaa koon, "Nenh koonaa'," neeł'ehedednee eetl'ekk. Eeydee, "Yoonaane looloolooloo-loo," nee eehoo. At'eeyło ełkeeh doldoye, koon ghedeyenh eehoo. Huyeł hʉn kk'ʉdaa koon kk'ʉdaa, "Nenh koonh," yegge denaa koon ehednee eetl'ekk.

Then he heard someone say to another, "How about you?" The other one sang, *"Yoonaane looloolooloo-looloo,"* but to no avail. Apparently it was the boreal owl. He tried to make medicine, but it had no effect. Then K'etetaalkkaanee heard them say to someone else, "Why don't you try?"

Huyeł hʉn, "Seeyaan' setlee' hoolaanh kk'e deseheł'aanh hu haa bedzege naal'on sets'e etlaak'ehenołteeł. Seeyaan' setlee' hoolaanh kk'e deseheł'aanh hu haa bedzege hʉkk'e naal'on sets'e etlaak'ehenołteeł," ts'edetaalnee'.

"As if I were the only powerful one, they are offering me a bag of oil filled to the navel. As if I were the only powerful one, they are offering me a bag of oil filled to the navel."[5]

4. The speaker meant that he could not help the mink; K'etetaalkkaanee's power was too great.

5. Bags used to be made out of skins, and a bag of oil was considered quite valuable. A bag

"Go hełde seeyaan' huyeł eseneyh kk'e deseheł'aanh hu haa sets'etlaak'ehenołteeł," nee ts'en'. Go huyeł deneyh. Huyeł hun benok'eetaadledzeyh. Benok'eetaadledzeyh. Huyeł ts'eenaadlegeet. At'eeyło, negoodzeghe. Yegge gheel eey hootl'ełts'e dedneehee.

That was his way of saying, "They are offering me a bag of oil filled to the navel, as if I were the most powerful one here." He was a powerful medicine man. While he was singing, light began to flash on K'etetaalkkaanee. It shined on him, on and off. K'etetaalkkaanee began to be afraid. Apparently it was a great horned owl chanting. You know what a loud voice he has.

Huyeł hun yoodo' huts'e, "Heee'! Sekoy hootl'ełts'e buhdeegheeneek eenhde kk'odehun' yooneets'e too kk'e donok'ot'oł ts'e Taakk'oołt'aan ts'aatokkaał. Eedenh yaan' yugh neetoneyhtl łonh," yełnee.

Then the owl said, "Oh! My grandchild is badly hurt, but when the sun rises over the water tomorrow *Taakk'oołt'aan*[6] will come out from around the bend upriver. Only he will be able to help her."

Doo', bekk'aa hoolneek. Eenaadlegeet. Hoozoonhts'e beł ts'eneelteelaa.

Doo', K'etetaalkkaanee had been discovered. He was frightened. He did not sleep well that night.

Dehoon kk'udaa nodo' needze taalkkaanh, kk'odehun'. Too kk'e donok'ot'oł go debezegheenee' ts'en'. Kk'odehun' te gheel eey yooneets'e too kk'e donok'et'oyh saanh te uhdehoot'aa. Kk'udaa nodo' needze ts'okkaał.

The next morning he started paddling downriver again. As the sun rose, it shone on the surface of the water, just as they had predicted. You know how the sun shines on the water early in the morning in the summer. He paddled downstream.

---

filled to the navel would have been about half full. The speaker was indirectly asking his spirit-helpers for aid. In effect, he was saying to them, "I've been given something valuable by these people who have faith in my medicine power, so please don't let me down."

6. *Taakk'oołt'aan* means "resident of *Taakk'oołt*," a distant place upriver. The owl is referring to K'etetaalkkaanee here by his place of origin.

Ts'ʉhʉ kk'ʉdaa, "Yooneets'e ees kk'ʉdaa ts'aats'eneekkaanh," nodo hʉts'e hednee eetl'ekk. Ło'ts'e ts'enelget. Ts'ʉh hʉyeł-deneyhne eet daadletl'ee.

Nodo' needze ts'okkaał. Kk'ʉdaa dotlee hebetlee neegho-ts'eneekkaanh.

"Heee'! Sołt'aanh bʉgh hootse-nenh ʉhdeegheeneek. De gen koon det'aanh?" beeznee.

Eet ts'edletonh. Ts'enleget. Notlee neeghots'eneekkaanh. Huyeł hʉn, "Heee'! Nedaats'e hogho dodʉhnee. O tlaa zee sʉgh nʉkk'ʉdʉhkkoyaa'," beeznee. Eey heł koon nelget.

Nonʉhts'e kk'ʉdaa nʉkk'ʉhe-yedeekkonh. Kk'ʉdaa go ts'eyee ts'eldo dehoon yʉh beyeł kk'e dok'ets'edlekooł. Ts'ʉh yedełdooł dehoon go dek'e kk'odenotl'en yekk'aa ts'aadeneeton yeł nodee-naaltset. Yedeteeł'eel de yʉh degge daanoneełtset. Ts'ʉh naa-degge, "Dzot no'oolst'eet! Dzot no'oolst'eet! Nʉgh ʉdenh ent'aa eey deseeloh. Nʉgh ees ʉdenh. Nʉgh ees benyeet," yełnee dehoon

K'etetaalkkaanee heard them saying, "There he is coming around the bend, from upriver." He was very frightened because the people there were medicine people.

He paddled downstream and landed his canoe by the village.

"A very dear woman is hurt. Who is it that came?" they asked him.

K'etetaalkkaanee remained in his canoe. He was afraid. He stayed where he had landed. "Well, I don't know if I will be able to help. Why don't you bring her down to me on a stretcher," he said. It serves him right that he was afraid.

They carried her down the bank on a stretcher. Still sitting in the canoe, he covered his head and the mink woman's wound with a cloth. He blew on the wound and pulled out the shaft of his arrow. Before he knew what had happened, the mink jumped up and rushed up the bank, saying, "I got my leg back! I got my leg back! He's the one. I recognize his nose," she said while running up

nodegge… Doo', nodegge. Neɫ'e-daanok'ets'eedeyeɫ. Haanozeel-gheɫ. Eet heɫde tlede eelelaa. Eeyet kk'ʉdaa koon hʉyeɫ oolkaanh.

the bank. *Doo'*, she rushed up the bank. K'etetaalkkaanee quickly pushed off the bank and fled. He fled in fear. He did not spend the night there, but paddled away.

Dotson' Deghuskk'oze Etlyeł Denh
When He Grabbed Raven's Beak

Ts'ʉh kk'ʉdaa nodo' koon nee-dze ts'okkaał. Go eet neełlot de hʉt'aan yetaatl-'aanh? Nedaats'e ghulaa'. Ts'e go kk'ʉdaa go ede det'aanh ts'e koon kk'ʉdaa debee-doy nooyee naaghedegges. Ts'ʉh doogh hogholedlenh degheel de-beedoy nooyee gheegges. Ts'ʉh nodo' nokkokk'e taalyo. Ts'ʉh go ede det'aan ts'e netlaahok'ets'ede-naadletuł. Ts'ʉh eet ts'etltaanh. Degge daadebet ts'e etltaanh dehoon bentseyh delzees. Kk'ʉdaa eeyet ts'etltaanh.

Aadots'e hʉn baats not'ʉhtl. Eet degge daadebet ts'e ts'ełtaa---nh.

Huyeł hʉn, "Doyeh k'etltaanh. Doyeh k'etltaanh," ts'edetaalnee', go baats.

Huyeł hʉn bekk'e hʉts'e hʉn koon, "Eee'! Hʉdok'edee beleel leełtson?" dodeenee. Go "dok'edee beget leełtson?" dodeenee beeznee ts'en'. At'eeyło koon k'eget yaan' tohon' ts'en'.

Once again, he was paddling downriver. He must have seen a raven from far away. As usual, he landed and dragged his canoe back into the woods. He dragged his canoe into the woods at the upper end of a sandbar on the edge of the river, and he began to walk down on the sandbar. As he had done before, he gave himself a nosebleed and threw himself down. He lay motionless on his back, his nose bleeding. He lay there as if he were dead.

A sea gull was flying upriver toward him. He just lay there on his back, motionless.

The sea gull started saying, "There's something dead below. There's something dead below."

A voice came from behind the sea gull. "Hey! Did you notice its smell?" it asked. "Did you notice whether it was rotten?" Apparently it said that because it liked only spoiled food.[1]

1. It was Raven.

"Oho'," beeznee. Go baats'en-leget, go baats. Dehoon go yʉh ʉdenh tlaahu kk'ʉdaa heɫ naaye-gge gheel bʉgh nok'ets'eghee-kkʉyh. At'eeyɫo ɫo dotson' go deneeyee go k'ʉhkk'e not'ʉhdlee. Dehoon baats heɫde k'eeɫtaanh.

"Yes," the sea gull replied. The sea gull was afraid of it. However, the raven was so greedy that it was the first one to land. Apparently the raven had come up from behind, while the sea gull found K'etetaalkkaanee.

Kk'ʉdaa bʉgh nok'ets'eghee-kkʉyh. Ts'ʉh no'o ts'eneeɫ'aanh. O do'o ts'etltaanh. Denaantseyh ts'aalekkongheeleen' ɫonh, ts'e yʉh dehoot'aa. Yoo'en bets'e netlaats'el-kkooyh, netlaats'elkkooyh. "Tl'o-gho dok'edeet?" ts'oodnee. Tl'ogho yʉh ts'ootaadleyonh dehoon kk'ʉ-daa benogh tlaahu ts'eetaaltleɫ. Dehoon yedeghuskk'oze etlyeɫ. Zaadleggaakk dehoon nodegge, dedeghuskk'oze edeenh.

The raven landed near K'etetaal-kkaanee and looked at him. He sure looked dead. He looked as if his nose had been bleeding. The raven inspected him timidly, preparing to peck at him. "Is he really dead?" the raven wondered. Poised to fly off, the raven pecked at an eye with its beak.[2] Just as it pecked, K'etetaalkkaanee grabbed its beak. The raven said "GGAAKK!" and flew off without its beak.

"Hʉ! Nedaanh tl'eegho yeleel etltson, go ehe deyɫneeyee," ts'edetaalnee'. Dehoon baats gheel yoogh kk'ots'enaat'oh, go neget aa-haa. Kk'ʉdaa, "Nedaa', nedaa', eey sedeghuskk'oze," beeznee. "Setl'onone'oyh!"

The raven began to complain, "Huh! Did he really smell some-thing dead before he announced that?" The sea gull was flying around far away because it feared the raven. The raven begged K'etetaalkkaanee, "Give it to me, give it to me. Give me my beak! Give it back to me."

"Dotl-'aanh ts'en'? Nenh gheel eey baahaa senokk'ʉ ts'aak'etaalee-tlaatl eehu hee," beeznee gheelhee.

"Why should I? You are the one who was going to chop out my eye with it," K'etetaalkkaanee told

2. The *denaakk'e* verb *-tleɫ* actually means "to chop" rather than "to peck." It is used here metaphorically to relate the raven's beak to a man's axe.

"Nenh gheel eey baahaa seetelaa-leełghaan' eehuhee."

Ło'ts'eyʉh, "Setl'onon'oyh."

Nonoo' debeedoy ghʉ nooyee naaghedeyo. Ts'ʉh debeedoy ts'aa-noneegges. Nodo' needze taal-kkaanh.

Ło'ts'eyʉh bedozełneeyaa. "Nedaa' eey sedeghuskk'oze," beeznee. Ło'ts'eyʉh betleekk'e kk'ots'enaat'oh.

"Nenh gheel baahaa destaalee-leen' eehuhee. Dehe'en gheel eey desloghee," yełnee.

Ło'ts'eyʉh, "Nedaa', nʉgh nets'e nebaah taaghtltseeł," yełnee.

"Dodeenee," yełnee.

Nodo' t'aanh. Go "Nedaa', nedaa' eey sedeghuskk'oze," nee eehu ts'ʉh.

Nodo' needze ghekkaał. Huyeł hʉn yoodots'e hʉn tl'ogho yʉh yaats'en yʉh hʉlkk'ʉł dehoon yaa-ts'en yʉh hʉdenodetl'eestl. At'eeyło baats yeł dotson' yeł. Tl'ogho no-dots'e yʉh hebaahaa yʉh hʉkk'aa k'eeghedeł kk'e dehoneeł gheel-hee, go dotson'. Kk'ʉdaa dodeggu be-

him. "You are the one who was going to kill me."

"Give it back to me!" the raven begged repeatedly.

K'etetaalkkaanee walked into the woods where he had left his canoe, dragged it out, and started paddling downriver again.

The raven never stopped pleading with him. "Give it to me. Give me my beak," it told him. It flew around above him.

"You are the one who was going to hurt me with it. That is why I took it," he told the raven.

"Give it back or I will make war against you," the raven told him.

"Go ahead," he replied.

The raven flew off downriver having repeatedly begged him, "Give it to me. Give me my beak."

K'etetaalkkaanee continued to paddle downstream. Soon, on one side of the river, there was nothing but a white mass approaching him, while on the other side, a black mass was approaching. Apparently one side was a mass of sea gulls flying toward him, while the other

tleekk'e dehoon tl'eełten' aahaa yʉh nok'etaatlbaatl. Nok'etaalbeyhtl. Huyeł go dotson' tlaahu daadleggaagge nodo' kk'aaghe dodo' t'aanh. Detlekts'e nodo' zonh.

was a mass of ravens. The ravens formed what looked like a black cloud coming up from downriver. Just as one of the ravens was right above him, he shot it with an arrow. He began to shoot them down one by one. Then the raven said "GGAAKK!" and they all turned around and flew downriver. The sea gulls followed.

Ts'ʉh kk'ʉdaa doogh zo koon nonot'ʉhtl. Ts'ʉh, "Nedaa', eey sedeghuskk'oze'," yełnee eehoo. Ło'ts'eyʉh, "Nedaa', nʉgh nedogh notlaagheenaaghst'ʉhtl," yełnee.

After a while, the raven flew up to him again and begged him, "Give me back my beak," but it was to no avail. "Give it back or I will block your path with a canyon," the raven told him.

"Dodeenee," yełnee.

"Go ahead," K'etetaalkkaanee replied.

Nodo' t'aanh. Dehoon needze ts'okkaał. O yoogh neegho'ekkaayh gheelhee. Yoodo--- zo tlaa neełts'e taal'o. Yoogh tlaaloołyeet hʉlaaghe gheelhee. Tlaa neełts'e taal'o. Yegge hʉn hede'ot yeł neełts'e heyk'ent'ʉh. Ts'ʉh neełdeełgho notelguyh. Neełdeegho notelguyh.

It flew off downriver again. K'etetaalkkaanee continued to paddle downstream. He must have landed here and there. Far downstream there were steep cliffs on either side of the river. Probably it was to become a canyon. The bluff protruded on both sides. The raven and his wife were pulling on the bluffs, which were moving in and out like scissors. Each time they pulled, the bluffs closed in like scissors.

Nodo' needze ghekkaał. Kk'ʉdaa eet doneets'e ghekkaał. Netsoo tl'aaghedekkon ehok'edeedletseenh. Ts'ʉh yʉgh eedekk'aayh de

K'etetaalkkaanee continued to paddle downstream. Just before he got to the canyon cliffs, he turned himself into a *netsoo*

dodo' too yeets'e hoghaalkk'aayh. Doo', nonee zo bekk'aatl'ot.

tl'aaghedekkone'.[3] He slipped between the cliffs underwater and surfaced on the other side, resuming his normal shape. *Doo'*, the canyon was behind him.

Kk'ʉdaa ło'ts'eyʉh, "Setl'o-non'oyh."

The raven kept begging him, "Give me back my beak."

Kk'ʉdaa nodo' needze ghe-kkaał dehoon kk'ʉdaa ło'ts'eyʉh bedoyedełneeye. Kk'ʉdaa, "Nenh gheel eey baahaa destaaleeleen' eehuhee eenhde hʉyeł bekk'aa de'eent'aa daa' ghedehtl ts'en' sedoghe toghudaał," yełnee.

K'etetaalkkaanee continued to paddle downstream while the raven pleaded with him. "You are the one who was going to hurt me with it, but if you really want it back, make a herd of caribou cross in front of me," he told the raven.

"Eeydaa' yegge k'ʉhnotle ghe-baal soo'oo'," yełnee. Nodo' t'aanh.

"If I do, don't shoot the leader," the raven replied, and it flew off downriver.

Ts'e doogh needze ghekkaał. Needze ghekkaał. Huyeł dodo hʉn benotle yʉh ghedehtl ts'en bedzeyh. Go hełde neełkk'aayegge denghe-dolkʉh ts'e gheel ghulaa' ghedehtl ts'en' beeznee.

He paddled and paddled down-stream. A little way below, a herd of caribou began to cross the river. *Ghedehtl tsen'* refers to a herd of caribou of different sizes and ages, with the largest animals in the front and progressively smaller ani-mals toward the back of the herd.

Ts'ʉh kk'ʉdaa yʉgh neeghe-kkaał. Naaghel'uł dehoon yʉh yedoghe neeneekkaanh. Ts'ʉh go k'ʉhʉnotle ghebaal yʉh yee k'eenaatltl'eł, go tl'eełten' aahaa.

So he approached them. As they were swimming across, he paddled in front of them and took aim at the leader with a bow and arrow.

3. He turned into a creature the size and shape of a needle. *Netsoo tl'aaghedekkone'* literal-ly means "your grandmother's needle."

Huyeł zaadleggaakk dehoon yʉh bets'enh hots'enodebets. "Haa! Ho go k'ʉhʉnotleey soo' beesnee denh!" daadeyoh.

The raven cried "GGAAKK !" and flew out from inside of the caribou as fast as it could, screaming, "Hey! Didn't I tell him not to shoot the leader?"

Toyołtaał. Soohoonaaneey koon go toyołtaał dehoon go yedeghuskk'oze yʉh yetleekk'e dol'onh. Go kk'o'eełebaaye, go dotson'. Ts'ʉh kk'ʉdaa koon nonee hʉts'e koon benozeenaałt'ʉkk eetl'ekk. Dehoon baats yʉh yetleekk'e hʉts'e detaalnee', benotle.

The leader floated in the water, dead. Of course K'etetaalkkaanee had done it on purpose. He then placed the raven's beak on the floating caribou. Ravens do not swim. K'etetaalkkaanee kept on going, and he heard the raven flying above the caribou in a circle. The sea gulls covered the caribou before the raven could get to it.

Nonee hʉts'e kk'ʉdaa nosaałeyenh eetl'ekk.

Again, K'etetaalkkaanee could hear the raven making medicine.

"Leghegekkoole. Leghegekkool denh. Nʉggʉ duhł'aanh eey duhł'aanee," ts'edetaalnee'.

"I do not float. I do not float. Why don't you do what you must on the ground?" the raven sang.[4]

Nodo yʉh honokkghee'oy yʉh netoyedegheełtaanh de neeghotoyeeneełtaanh. At'eeyło go toyołtaał daa' yʉh baats yenotle k'ʉhdeetoheeł gheelhee, dʉhʉgh yʉh yenee aahaa.

Soon the caribou washed up against a sandbar (but still away from the shore). If it had kept floating, the sea gulls would have devoured it before the raven could have reached it. Of course the raven was worried about it

Ts'ʉh kk'ʉdaa eet dodo' koon kk'ʉdaa ghekkaał.

Once again, K'etetaalkkaanee paddled downriver.[5]

4. This was the raven's medicine song. He wanted to cause the caribou carcass to come ashore so that he could retrieve his beak and eat the meat.

5. K'etetaalkkaanee took some meat from the other caribou that he had killed.

Boogh Tleeɫtl'en Bʉgh Neeghodenaaneeyo Denh

Where His Older Brother's Skull Came Ashore to Him

Needze ghekkaał. Ghekkaał, ghekkaał. Yoodo hʉts'e ts'aaneekkaanh de yoodo hʉn koon k'ek'eeze'oh. Dehoon nodo' needze ghekkaał.

He paddled and paddled and paddled downstream. He came around a bend, where he saw someone tanning a skin. He paddled downriver toward her.

Dehoon donłts'e doneets'e ghekkaał dehoon gheel, "Heee'! Bezo yooneets'e ts'aats'eneekkaanh hu ło notodeedetl'eets." Yegge hʉn go k'eleł nozeghee'ʉh. Aałnots'edenłtseet. Et'eeyło denaa leł go yełlaaghee. Donggʉ hʉn saanh yeh hoolaanh. Kk'ʉdaa neeghoneekkaanh.

As he approached, the woman who was tanning the skin said, "Hey! No wonder the water turned black. Someone came out from around the bend." Quickly, she removed the skin that she was tanning from the post it was hanging over and rolled it up. Apparently she had been tanning a human skin. Behind her was a smokehouse. He landed there.

Ts'ʉh, "Hee! Denaa edenh de debaa koon det'aanh." Ło'ts'eyʉh besots'eey aahaa. Kk'ʉdaa, "Nʉgh k'etegheehon'," beeznee. Kk'ʉdaa doogh baabe bʉgh neets'eneelo, nelaan ggunh yeł. Doogh hʉn koon tlooghaa naał beteghenaadedzaakk.

"Oh good! There are hardly any people around here. Who is it that came?" she said with great joy. "You're going to eat," she told him. She set out some food for him. There was some dried meat, and he saw some long, human hairs dried onto the meat.

Ts'ʉh, "Doneets'e et'eghł neeghonskkaanh de nok'aaghesdon' ts'e ees go sedzogh dehoot'aa'aa," yełnee.

He told her, "I stopped and ate upriver, so I'm not very hungry."

"Aa oho' eeydaa' ts'aale," nee.

Doogh bek'ets'oonaatlłon' eehu ts'ʉh doogh ło'ts'eyʉh dots'oolaah. Dehoon daangge nooyee saal'ots. Huyeł hʉn doogh hʉn yʉh nooyee tleeghedegges. Ts'ʉh ehu daangge gheel taalyo. Daangge ghehoł.

Huyeł dʉnggʉ hʉn benh daal'onh. Kk'ʉdaa eet hedeeyo. Eet lehaanh. Go ʉhdon huyeł deneyh hu noghodeneyhtl. Ts'ʉh eet lehaanh.

Nedaaghe aanłets'e taaghe kkaatl'oh hʉn koon denaa tlee' neeghodenohoł. Kk'ʉdaa donłts'e bets'e neeghoyedenaaneeyo.

Dehoon gheel, "Yeey'! Tl'aaa', dont'aanh koonh?" beeyłnee.

Yeneeł'aanh. Huyeł go hʉn koon boogh t'aanh koon benotle heyedeeyoy tlee', ło go dedneeyee. At'eeyło hʉkk'e neebełyeeneełtaanh denh. Ts'ʉh eet ts'elaatlghaanh denh. At'eeyło hebets'eldaał. Dehoon nonggʉ benh ghʉ hʉn koon yʉh k'etlee' taah dodenaat'onh.

"Tl'aaa', tlaa zee dent'aanh ts'e yegge eenaaleetaanh daa' le'on

"Oh, okay. It's all right then," she replied.

She tried to feed him. She could not do enough for him. He walked back into the woods to relieve himself. A well-worn path led back into the woods. He began to follow it. He walked along.

Then he came upon a little lake. He walked out of the woods and went up to it. He knew about that place, having dreamed of it before. He stood there.

Then he saw a human head coming toward him on the bottom of the lake. It came ashore and approached him.

It said to him sadly, "Oh no! My dear, what are you doing here?"

He looked at it. Then he recognized the head as that of one of his older brothers who had left home before him. That place was as far as his medicine power had brought him. He had been killed there. Apparently many people had been eaten and their skulls had filled the lake.

"Dear one, even though it may not help, when you go to bed, lay a

nedzaay kk'e dodeneeghoo'oł," yełnee.

rock over your heart," the head told him.

Kk'ʉdaa notlen ts'aanotaałeyo. Ts'egheetsaah, go doogh tlee' negheeł'aan'. Ts'aanots'eet'ots. Dotlee saanh kkʉno hedonots'eet'ots. Huyeł denaagheneedee! Dodʉggʉ hʉn koon bebeedoy yʉh łet yekk'e'oodletl'oon'. Hets'etltl'oonh. Ts'ʉh gheel doogh zee ts'eldo.

K'etetaalkkaanee started to walk back to the camp. Having seen his older brother's head, he cried. He came back out of the woods to the camp. He went into the smokehouse. What the devil! To his surprise, his canoe was tied to the racks. It was lashed down under the roof of the smokehouse. He sat around, not knowing what else to do.

Dehoon kk'ʉdaa dzaan hʉgheelet. Ts'ʉh kk'ʉdaa heenaaltaanh.

The day had passed. They began to get ready for bed.

Go yʉh ło'ts'eyʉh, "Sekkun' laaghe," beeznee ts'e yʉh dots'oolaah.

She could not do enough for him, saying, "You're going to be my husband."

Ts'ʉh henaaltaanh dehoon go le'on dedzaay tleekk'e dodenaal'onh. Dehoon beł hok'ets'edeenaadledaakk.

After they went to bed, he placed a flat rock over his heart and pretended to go to sleep.

Degge daanots'eelneek. Ts'ʉh donł nok'eesaalkk'onh eetl'ekk. Nok'ets'ekk'o. "Yeey', k'edeeteey desloh," nee dehoon genee ghulaa' aadaadlet'otl eetl'ekk. Kk'ʉdaa nonots'e bets'e nonots'ot'ustl eetl'ekk dehoon ts'eghetełnoyaa. Go ts'eltaanh de yʉh denaa'etl'ozaałetlut.

The woman got up quietly. He could hear her begin to sharpen something. Indeed, she was sharpening something. He heard a cutting sound as she said, "Oh, I overdid it." He lay still as he heard her coming back over to him. She stood over him and then sat down on him as hard as she could.

Hʉdaadlets'eekk dehoon denaadʉgh zoltl'et. Nedaats'e ghulaa' haahaa denaa eghonh. Ts'e go hʉtl'odedetlut, go saay kk'aant'aay yeł. Ts'ʉhʉ denaadʉgh zołtl'et.

Something squeaked and she fell off him, unconscious. I don't know how she killed people, but she sat on them with something like a knife. She fell over, unconscious.[1]

"Hmhmhmh!" ts'ednee ts'e doogh ts'aanohok'ezeellet. "He go ło ʉhdon yeekk'e nohooldlet," ts'ednee.

K'etetaalkkaanee said, "Hmhmhmh!" and pretended to wake up. "Oh, is it morning already?"

Go sołt'aanh doogh doghunaah.

The woman acted strangely, not knowing what to do.

Doogh mendogho holeł, "Hu! Atlebaa'! Abaa setlee'. Go ło hʉnk'uh dotaalnee'?" nee gheelhee. "K'edeeteey hʉnlek'uh dehoon beł neeghegetenh ts'e ees go setlee'... Ho eey kk'odon doneets'e needze gheskkaał de, aanee t'aanh too naakk'ʉdle ets'aadaaneełlenh. Too naakk'ʉdle ghesenoon' daa' soo'u," nee. Kk'ʉdaa, "Too soho ʉkkʉnho haa'," beeznee.

Later in the morning K'etetaalkkaanee said, "Whew! It's hot! My head hurts. Why is the weather so hot, anyway?" he asked. "I got a headache from sleeping in the heat. Yesterday, when I was paddling downriver, I saw a stream of cold water flowing into the river. Maybe if I drink some cold water it will help," he said. Then he told her, "Why don't you go up there to get some water for me?"

Kk'ʉdaa ło'ts'eyʉh go dots'oolaah. "Oho', heen'," ts'ednee. Ts'ʉh too ghenee ts'etlyel yeł gheel notlen aanoo' hʉyoze neets'enee'ots degheel, "Nedaadenh? Heen', nedaadenh?" beeznee.

She would do anything for him. "Okay, honey," she said. She grabbed something to put water in, rushed down the bank, went a short distance upriver, and asked him, "Where? Honey, where?"

1. The blade was attached to her body. Evidently she broke it as she sat down on the rock.

"Nonee noo' hu t'aasee. Nonee noo' hu ent'aay dehaasnee," yełnee.

"Way up there. Farther upriver is where I mean," he answered her.

Yegge ede noo'ts'e k'ets'e nonolnoyh ts'e tl'ooł k'eełekk'ee nełtsuk, go nodeggu debeedoy. Kk'ʉdaa, "Heen' nedaadenh?" beeznee.

She kept asking where it was, and each time she turned her back, he cut one of the ropes that bound his canoe to the smokehouse. Once again, she said, "Honey, where?"

Ts'ʉh, "Nonee t'aasee. Nonee eesee."

"Way up there. Up there."

Noo'ts'e k'ets'e nonoghelnoł dehoon koon nok'enaatltsut. Kk'ʉdaa yoonee naa' hu needok'eghedodenoł. Dehoon kk'ʉdaa ts'aa'et'eey nonaatltsut.

She turned her back to him again and he cut another rope. By that time she was far upriver, still asking where he meant. Then he cut the last rope.

Naagheghʉłtl dehoon ts'etlyeł. Go ts'aa deeloy et'aanee. Ts'ʉh notlee yʉh too aayedaatlt'usk de yeyee gheltluh.

He caught the canoe as it fell. He probably did not have many things to put back in it. He rushed down to the water, threw the canoe into the water, and jumped in.

Nonee, "Haa! Enaa sekkun'!" Noneets'e hʉts'en'. Nodo' needze taadledzeł. "Enaa sekkun' nekk'e tok'etl'enhghesebaatl," nee ts'e nonee hʉts'e too daatlkots eetl'ekk. Dehoon nodo' nedaats'e neek'eeldzeł.

He heard her upriver, saying, "Hey! My dear husband!" He heard her following him. He began to paddle downriver as fast as he could. "My dear husband, I'm going into the water behind you," she said. He heard the water splashing behind him as he paddled. He paddled as fast as he could a long time.

Needze ghelghełtl, dehoon noye' koon degheeł'aan'. Ts'ʉh go

As he went downriver, he caught some beaver, but he was

k'edeeteey hʉgho'eetenaaltsonh beł aahaa dent'aa. Ts'ʉh go, "Tlaa go k'eeługh kk'e k'edeetaaghgeleyhtl," nee dehʉgh nokkokk'e neeghoneekkaanh. Eet yʉh hobełyegheełtaanh. Hootl'ełts'e gheel beł ts'eenaadledaakk. Yoogh yeekk'e nohooldlet gheelhee. Yeekk'e nobełk'ets'enaadletenh.

Ts'aanaaghedeleł dehoon, "Haa! Łoghʉne. Ho k'aagheslaak denh," yeneelenh.

Ts'ʉh doogh ghetaalnonh. Huyeł Huh! go hʉn koon gen tseł bekot'e ełetlaakk, et'eeyło go sołt'aanh.

Go hʉn koon noye' leł ts'ede tl'es bekk'e dołetlaakk. Dokk'ʉ nek'e yʉh ts'ede etltseenh, o go magic.

Eet kk'ʉdaa yelaatlghaanh. Kk'ʉdaa eet dodo' koon kk'ʉdaa neek'ono'eedekkaanh. Ts'ʉh yoogh ghekkaał.

very tired from lack of sleep. He landed on a sandbar and thought, "I'll just take a quick nap." He fell asleep there and slept soundly. The entire night must have passed. He slept the entire night.

As he woke up, he thought, "Oh, yes! I have to skin the beaver that I caught."

He moved. Ugh! Something wet and slimy was sleeping next to him. It was that woman.

He was lying under a blanket made of raw, wet beaver skins. How fast she had skinned the beavers and made a blanket! She had done it with magic.

That is when he killed her. Then he paddled off downriver again. He paddled along.

Sołt'aanh Betl'ots'eyegheełtaanh Ghenee Nesoogheetleyh

He Made a Grave for the Girl Who Had Been Given to Him

Ghekkaał, ghekkaał, ghekkaał. Kk'ʉdaa koon yoogh ghekkaał. Huyeł hʉn yoodo hʉn zaadletl'ee de hʉts'e ts'aaneekkaanh. Ts'ʉh nodo' eet needze gheekkaanh. Ts'ʉh doogh tolyo. At'eeyło neełkkun' kkaa hededenaa' kkaa yeł yoogh saanh hʉtlenh ghʉ heldo. Hʉtlen ghʉ nehełneyh. Ts'ʉh kk'ʉdaa heyek'egheełon'. Ts'e doogh ledo.

He paddled and paddled and paddled. Once again he was paddling along. He paddled around the bend and came upon a camp. He paddled up to it and went up the bank. A man and wife were living there with their children. They were fishing. They fed him. He stayed there for a while.

Huyeł hʉn, "Hu nedaaghe hʉts'enh koon denaats'e denaa hoodoo'ʉ denh. Nedaaghe koon ghekkaal det'aanh? Nʉgh ees denaahʉdnaa' kk'ʉdaa neekkʉno hooto'oł eenee' zeeyʉh ledo de nedaats'e ghekkaal koon det'aanh?" yełnee. Go haahaa, "Kk'ʉdaa nʉgh denaadenaa' eenłkoot," yełnee ts'en'. Eeydee ghʉ todo'. Ts'ʉh denaaghʉ kk'otodeneyh yełnee dʉhʉghʉnh.

"There are hardly any people around here. Where did he come from? How did he happen to come here? We have a daughter here who is still not married. How did he happen to come here?" the man said. That was his way of asking K'etetaalkkaanee to marry his child. He wanted him to marry her so that K'etetaalkkaanee could provide for them.

Ts'ʉh eeydee ghʉ taaldo'. Yoogh ts'aa neełlotts'e eet gheedo'ee. "Seyeł kk'oneedekkaayh," go de'ot ełnee, go sołt'aanh.

K'etetaalkkaanee began to stay with her. He probably had not stayed very long when he told his wife, this girl, "Come travel with me."

Benee neeyeeneeyo, go sołt'aanh. Kk'ʉdaa nodo' aado' yoogh

The girl got into the canoe behind him. He paddled down-

neeneekkaanh. Degheel tlaa neeghoneekkaanh.

Ts'ʉh, "Tlaa gonh daaso'ʉstl," yełnee.

Ts'ʉh naangge taahel'ots. Tl'odoggʉ haahel'ots. Ts'ʉhʉ doogh ts'ebaa ken ghʉ gheel genee ghulaa' taatltseen'. Hʉłtsee. "Tlaa eey gonh haanaaneendo haaa'," yełnee.

Ts'ʉh eet hʉyee gheeyo. Ts'ʉh haanaaneedo. Huyeł gheel edetʉgh de'eełtaa'aa.

"Oho'," nee.

Ts'ʉh go dosts'eł'aanh yeneelenh. Hʉyo ede needoy gheelhee.

Ts'ʉh kk'ʉdaa yoogh koon tl'ee yʉgh kk'o'eedeneeyh. Ts'ʉh kk'ʉdaa koon, "Hodee, tlaa eey beyee nondoyaaa'," yełnee. Nonee yʉh hʉkk'aatl'o haanaaneedo ts'e kk'ʉdaa dehooloh.

Ts'ʉh go yet yʉh yoogh yelooł ghʉ k'edaaneeyeł gheelhee. Doyeeloh eehu yelaatlghaanh. Ts'ʉh eet yʉh haanaaneedo, go yeghenee

river, going a short distance. He paddled ashore.

"Let's get out here for a while," he told her.

They went up the bank, up to the top of the bank. He began to make something at the foot of a spruce tree. He made an enclosure. "Sit here and lean back against the tree," he told her.

She went inside the enclosure and leaned back against the tree, but it was not the right size for her.

"Okay," he said.

What did she think he was doing? She probably was not very smart.

He resumed working on it. Then he said, "Okay, why don't you sit in it one more time." He made it so that she could sit comfortably against the wall of the enclosure.

Then he must have stabbed her in the throat. He killed her in some way. The body was still leaning against the tree in the *soos* that he

soos etltseenh denh. Go hełde yoo-ghedon kk'edonts'ednee huyeł neeł'eneeholneyh ts'ednee ts'en'.

had made for her.[1] It is said that they used to bury each other in this way long ago and in Story Time.

Yoogh haał yee kk'e dehoot'aa de huhułtseeyh. Ts'uh eet huyee haaneełhenleyaayh. Go kk'udaa haahaa kk'eł neeł'aahelneyh ts'en'.

They built lean-tos, as we do for traps, and put each other into them. That is how they buried each other.

Uhdeyeeloh. Ts'uh aado' huyoze neeneekkaanh. Ts'uh go ede det'aanh ts'e debeedoy nooyee gheegges. Ts'uhu kk'aaghe ts'aa-no'eedeyo. Ts'uh dotlee donee too tleekk'e tenaal'oy ghaaghedeeyo. Ts'uh eeydee tleekk'e oodlek'ee---t. Hok'oodol'aan'. Aanoo' nohun-le'eeyh.

That is what he did to her. Then he went a little farther down-stream. As usual, he dragged his canoe back into the woods. He walked back out of the woods. He walked upriver a short distance and climbed into a tree that extended out over the river. He stretched out on it. He was watch-ing. He kept checking upriver.

Huyeł yooneets'e zo kk'udaa ts'aats'eneekkaanh. At'eeyło neeł-lots'e hebaaholeł. Ts'uh hebekk'aa ts'egheekkaanh, go sołt'aanh beto'. Huyeł gheel aants'e aaneets'e ghe-kkaał. Huyeł aado hun eet hutaatl-'aanh.

Soon someone paddled out from around the bend. Apparently the girl's father was looking for them because they had been gone a long time. He crossed the river as he paddled downstream. Then he saw the enclosure.

"Yeey'! Sedenaa' dokk'u soo' deheyeeloh hu yoodo zo yeghenee nesoogheeł'o." Go K'etetaalkkaa-nee eelaatlghaał beeznee duhughunh, nee gheelhee. Go beyee nehooldlet ts'uh.

"Oh no! How quickly he made a grave for my child." This was his way of saying that he intended to kill K'etetaalkkaanee. He was furious.

1. A *Soos* is a circular lean-to that was used long ago for burials. It was built either against a tree using the trunk as a main support, or out in the open. The body was placed within the lean-to in a sitting position.

Noneets'e zo yetleets'en ootaalkkaanh go bekk'aa taaghskkaał yełnee dʉhʉghʉnh. Ts'ʉh gheel soot'e hʉyeł deneyh kk'aant'aa gheelhee. Ts'e go dotloogh doneets'e dehoon kk'ʉdaa toyołtaał. Needze toyołtaał.

Ts'e go edenk'e tl'eedegge hʉneeł'aanee? Go dets'oodenee ts'en' doyeggu taah hʉneeł'aanh. Soot'e yʉh gen ghulaa' taatl-'aanh kk'aant'aa. Doogh kk'ełts'e eet hʉneeł'aanh. Huyeł doyehts'e kʉn koon taah beyeneeł'aanh.

Ts'ʉh go baaneyh gheelhee genee eehu etlyeł. Ts'ʉh tl'ogho yʉh naayegge yʉh eeydee yeł yʉh taanaaltl'eł. Honotoyegheełtuts.

Ts'ʉh dodo' debeedoy naa'etlyeł. Doogh hʉneeł'aanh eehoo eenh go dets'oodnee ts'e tl'ee degge tleetełt'oyaa. Kk'ʉdaa nonoo' koon neeno'eedekkaanh. Ode degheet'aa'. Ts'ʉh kk'ʉdaa go, "Tlaa eey hełde soo' koon notaaghege'eeł," yeneelenh.

Kk'ʉdaa koon go kk'ʉdaa tl'ogho yʉh yokko hʉneeł'aanh. Dehoon gheel baahaa honotosetotltaalaa yełneey le'on taaneets nok'enaaneehooł, le'on neteekk'ee.

He started to paddle downriver past K'etetaalkkaanee, planning to follow him. He must have sensed that K'etetaalkkaanee was nearby because he stopped paddling and drifted in the water.

Didn't he look up? K'etetaalkkaanee willed him to look down into the water. He thought he saw something, so he looked over the side of his canoe and saw K'etetaalkkaanee looking up at him from the water.

Then the man grabbed his spear from behind him and dove into the water. Soon he floated back up to the surface.

The man went downstream and retrieved his canoe. He looked around where he thought he had seen him, but nothing was there. Just as K'etetaalkkaanee had willed, the man never looked up. He paddled back upstream and waited for a while. "I wonder if I will see him again," he thought.

He looked around for him again. So that he would not float up to the surface so quickly this time, he tied two rocks together. He floated in his canoe, looking

Ts'ʉh kk'ʉdaa ehu toyołtaał. At'eeyło koon nodʉggʉ deyenenh kuh deyoodnee ts'en'. Ahu toyołtaał. Go ede neenotobełtaayh de neenotobołtaał dehoon nedaa doyeh hʉn beyeneeł'aanh. Go le'on neteekk'ee yetaaneets nok'enaaneehool dekk'uł nedengheełdaatl. Dehoon noyegge...

down into the water, as the big medicine man, K'etetaalkkaanee, had willed him to do. He drifted along. He kept drifting to the same place. Then he saw K'etetaalkkaanee looking up from below again. He grabbed the rocks that he had tied the rope around, threw the rope over his neck, and jumped in the water.

Taaghedeluk. Doo', honotodenaa'eełtaalaa. Daats'e gheel go heghe'en deyenyoo yoogh debaa ghʉ kk'oheedeneeyh tʉh taah hedeyeege heenotl-'aanee tl'ok yee eenhdenh. Go hełde eet yʉh hʉkk'e naal'onh go denaa dehe'en. Grandpa gheelaa' ees tl'ogho ʉhts'e ts'ohoodeegheełt'e. Ts'ʉh go hełde koon ʉhts'e hʉltsee ts'e gheelhee. Ʉhts'e k'ehegheenołe dʉhʉghʉnh.

He was pulled under by the rocks. *Doo'*, he did not come back up. This is why, when medicine people are working on someone, they instruct that person not to look at his own reflection, even in a pan. It is because of what happened in this story. My late grandpa did not like his patients to see their own reflection when he worked on them. The practice was being established for the future. Looking at the reflection could have a negative effect.

Doo', dekk'uł nele'ondengheełdaatl. Nonaaghdeyo. Ts'ʉh kk'ʉdaa nodo' debeedoy ghʉ neeno'eedeyo. Ts'ʉh kk'ʉdaa ʉhts'e haahaa koon kk'ʉdaa go sołt'aanh laatlghaanh, go beto' koonh. Ts'ʉh kk'ʉdaa yoogh eet dodo' koon ghekkaał. Needze ghekkaał.

Doo', this man killed himself by tying rocks around his neck and jumping into the water. K'etetaalkkaanee came down from the tree and went back to his canoe. That is how he killed the girl and her father. Then, once again, he paddled downstream.

Boogh Tson' Gheneede Ghʉ Neekkaanh Denh

When He Came to His Enslaved Older Brother

Ghekkaał, ghekkaał. Kk'ʉdaa koon yoogh nodo' ts'aaneekkaanh. Huyeł hʉn yoodo hʉn hʉts'e dehoodeyoh. At'eeyło ło saanlaaghedoh. Kk'ʉdaa tl'ogho hʉtlenh ghʉ nelneyh. Kk'ʉdaa nodo' eet needze gheekkaanh. Denaa hoolaanh.

He paddled and paddled. Once again, he came out from around a bend. He came around the bend to a settlement where there were many people. Apparently it was a fish camp. The people were putting away lots of fish. He paddled to the camp. Many people were there.

Huyeł hʉn doogh beggenaa' een hʉn, "Onee'," yełnee. Ts'ʉh eet, "Ggenaa, k'etegheehon'," yełnee. Ts'ʉh kk'ʉdaa no'o eet neeheneedaatl. Huyeł denaa hoolaanh.

Then a friend said to him, "Come here! Friend, you are going to eat," he told him. Many people were gathered at the place where they were going to eat.

Gheel yʉh k'eełde yennok'eheetaałdeegee yoogh hebeldon' gheelhee. Ts'e go kkʉnotl'ohedaadletl'ee' degheenee' go Grandpa gheelaa' yʉgh nohʉlnek denh. Kk'ʉdaa nonł yenk'eheeheeyh. Ło'ts'e łookk'e nekogh enolneek.

They were all starting to eat. My grandpa used to say that they all sat in a circle. They ate. They had cooked a lot of fish.

Genee detlege yenheeheeyh. Huyeł yegge yeggenhyoze hʉn ekee hodelyoh. Nonł yenk'eedeeyh dehoonh. Yoogh go gen k'ek'el yee hetodetl'oo'.

While they were eating, a baby made a mess. What clothes did the babies have to wear?

Huyeł gheel hʉn, "Ho no'o tson' gheneet beghenee ʉkkʉ'ʉh'os," beeznee.

Somebody said, "Send for the person who cleans up such messes."

"Hudaa! Gen soo' koon doznee," yeneelenh. Ts'e doogh eet ledo. Go yenk'eheeheeyh dehoon saakkaay ekee hodelyoh.

Denaagheneede! Nedaa yegge do'ots'e hun koon boogh de'aat'on beghok'eghaalk'el yok'aa---l hunde koon ghehoł. Heee'! Yegge hun yugh neeneeyo ts'uh doogh de'aat'on k'el baagh huneeł'aanh. Huyeł gheel hun go k'ek'el gheel go neeł-ts'aatołk'ełdlaa, eenh go yuh k'edeeteey tlogeey aahaa gheel yuh etlaah gheelhee. Ts'e go doogh de'aat'on yedegheełk'el, tege aahaa hun, go yeggenhyoz huyee ts'aataatltaanh.

Dehoon hun benogh yegge nu'untootedaał, go K'etetaalkkaanee. Degge daaneełtset. Ts'uh yuh no'o yeggenhyoze etlyel yuh yeeltuł gheelhee. Doyeeloh eehu. Yelaatlghaanh. Huyeł k'ets'e neehooneelet. K'uhudeeghunh. Go saanlaaghedoh daadletl'eey detlege yuh ehudeeghunh. Doogh yeen' k'edogheełtaanh.

"Yee! Ketl'aa, kk'udaa huyaan' huk'ots'en setl'ok'elkek ts'e ent'aa yegge... Go ło dotaaghsneeł dehugh go saak'uhdeenghunh?"

At'eeyło ło koon boogh k'eden hukk'e neeneetaanh denh.

"I wonder what they mean," K'etetaalkkaanee thought. He just sat there. The baby had made a mess while the people were eating.

To his surprise, his pitiful older brother walked up wearing an old, dried up parka. Pieces had been torn from it. Oh dear! He walked up to the baby and looked for a piece he could tear from his parka. A skin is not easy to tear, but this one was so old and dry that it tore easily. He tore off a piece and began to clean the baby with it.

When K'etetaalkkaanee saw this, tears flowed from his eyes. He jumped up and kicked the baby or did something to it. He killed it. There was a big fight and he killed everybody. He killed everybody at the fish camp. The only person he spared was his brother.

"Oh, no! My younger brother, that was the only way I could get food. What am I going to do now that you have killed everyone?"

Apparently that was as far as his other older brother had

Kk'ʉdaa hʉkk'e neebełyeeneełtaanh de ʉdeek'e yʉh baahaa hool'onh denh.

traveled. He had traveled that far in his spiritual journey before he met his demise.

Kk'ʉdaa, "Ts'aal senee neetegheehoł," yełnee.

K'etetaalkkaanee told him, "It's okay, you can sit behind me."

Kk'ʉdaa nodo' yeyeł neek'oneekkaanh. Neteehde yeyeł heghenolekkaanh. Hʉn dek'ets'ekkaah eehoo. Bebeedo' hedletenh kk'aa deyoh. Ło'ts'eyʉh dek'ekkaah eehoo.

His brother sat behind him and they took off downriver. He went around two bends with his brother. Then he could not go any farther; he paddled and paddled but did not move. It was as if his canoe were frozen in place. He paddled and paddled, but to no avail.

Donggʉ neeghoneekkaanh. Ts'ʉh eet nok'ehodon'. Eet hegheedo'. Kk'ʉdaa kk'oyenee'eedeleet. Kk'ʉdaa hʉn doogh ghʉ taaltsaah.

He paddled ashore, where they ate and stayed awhile. K'etetaalkkaanee thought and thought. Then he began to cry for his older brother.

Dek'ek'eenteł k'eełekk'ee haadeneetonh. "Tlaa eey koon senee neenoneedoyh," yełnee. Koonkoon boogh benee neeno'eedeyo.

He removed one crosspiece from his canoe. "Okay, let's try again. Get behind me," he told his older brother. Once again, his brother got into the canoe behind him.

Yoogh do'eet'aa'aa ts'e koonkoon aado' eet heł koon heghenolekkaanh. Dehoon go ede det'aanh ts'e koon koon henodletenh kk'aa deyoh. Ło'ts'eyʉh dek'ekkaah eehoo. Tledo'eełkkaayaa.

He left and went around one bend without any difficulty. Then, as before, it was as if the canoe had frozen in place. K'etetaalkkaanee paddled in vain. The canoe was not going anywhere.

Kk'ʉdaa koon neeghonoheede-

They paddled ashore and

kkaanh. Kk'ʉdaa eet koon heghee-do'. Kk'ʉdaa k'eenteł k'eełekk'ee koon haanodeneetonh. Kk'ʉdaa k'eenteł neteekk'ee haadeneetonh.

stayed there awhile. Then he removed another crosspiece. He had removed two altogether.

Ts'ʉh kk'ʉdaa go ede det'aanh ts'e neek'ono'eedekkaanh. Yoogh do'eet'e ts'e aado' heghenolkkaanh. De dodo' hʉyeł koon heno'eenaałe-neyh. Ło'ts'eyʉh dek'ekkaah eehoo.

As he had done before, he set off paddling. They went around one bend. Then he was stuck again. He paddled and paddled, but went nowhere.

Kk'ʉdaa ło'ts'e nedaats'e ghulaa' dughunaah. Neeghono'eekkaanh. Ts'ʉh doogh oho baabe denloh. Eet hʉts'enh en notodekkaak. Yoogh notodok hʉyeł gheelhee.

He did not know what to do next. He paddled ashore and got some food for his brother. While there, K'etetaalkkaanee went out hunting in his canoe. Maybe he went hunting on foot too.

Doogh ghʉ gheetsaah. Ts'ʉh kk'ʉdaa doogh ghʉ haanodeede-kkaanh. Kk'ʉdaa et'eeyło hʉkk'e kk'ʉdaa boogh k'eełekk'ee koon neebełneełtaanh denh. Kk'ʉdaa nodo' koon haanodeedekkaanh.

K'etetaalkkaanee cried for his older brother.[1] Eventually, he left. That place was as far as his brother had traveled in his spiritual journey. Once again, K'etetaalkkaanee paddled downstream.

1. K'etetaalkkaanee's brother could not go any farther down the river. His medicine power was not strong enough to get him past that village, nor could he go back upriver. He was stuck in that place. All K'etetaalkkaanee could do was leave him plenty of food.

K'oyeedenaa Yoo
Little People

Ts'ʉh needze ghekkaał. Needze ghekkaał. Needze ghekkaał. Kk'ʉdaa saanh tl'oghots'e---n'. Dodo hʉn koon kk'ʉdaa saanlaaghedoh hoolaanh de hʉts'e koon kk'ʉdaa ts'aaneekkaanh. Nodo' eet neeghekkaał. Huyeł hʉn aanggʉ hʉn koon yʉh neheghedenoh eenh k'ʉhgaal yʉh k'etetl-'eeyaa kk'aant'aa.

He paddled and paddled downstream. It was late in the summer. Once again, he paddled around a bend to a fish camp. He was almost there. It looked as if the place was bustling with activity, but he could not see anyone.

Nodo eet hʉts'e ghekkaał. Neeghoghekkaał.

He paddled toward it and went ashore.

Huyeł hʉn yʉh denaa soo' deegudze. Yoogh yʉh hebaahaa yʉh nʉhʉdekk'unh kk'e dʉhʉt'aanh go helonh ts'en'.

Then he saw that they were tiny people. There were so many of them that they looked like a flame moving around.

Ts'ʉh notlee neeghoneekkaanh. Do'ooghe yʉh kk'ohedenaadeggoot dehoon, "Yeey'! Nʉgh kk'ʉdaa nots'ełneegeey nonol'uyhtl. Kk'ʉdaa tlaa eey odeek'e denaayeł eeydee eenoł'aan'. Nʉgh bek'ʉhłonh," beeznee. Ło'ts'eyʉh heyesots'eey aahaa. Doogh ło'ts'eyʉh yʉh genee ghulaa' baabe dooł kk'aant'aay gheel heyegheełon'. Eet hʉyeł ledo.

He landed on the beach. They were everywhere and were saying, "Hey! Remember that the *nots'ełneegeey* crosses here every day.[1] Maybe he could help us with it. Feed him," they said. They were very happy to see him. I don't know what they fed him. It was like dust. He stayed there with them.

Huyeł hʉn, "Oho', kk'ʉdaa yoonee

"Okay, the sun is almost up at

1. *Nots'ełneegeey* is the the little people's word for caribou. It means "one that is rarely seen."

ees eet neenok'ot'oł. Kk'ʉdaa nots'ełneegeey nonodebaayh denh," hednee ts'e do'oogh hebeyee hool-'onh gheelhee.

the place where the *nots'ełneegeey* usually crosses the river," they said, rushing about.

Nedaa aanots'e hʉn koon be-dzeyh hebaats'aadeeyo. "Nonots'e eesee! Kk'ʉdaa nonotodebaał," ts'edetaalnee'.

Soon a caribou came out to the river on the opposite bank and started to swim across. "There it is! It's going to cross the river again," someone shouted.

Kk'ʉdaa nonots'e naaghebaał. Eenh gheel beyetaatl-'aanh daa' kkʉnonodetodebaał kk'aant'aa. Ts'ʉh gheel yedeetaalkkaanh. Ts'e go daahenaah ts'e go ehdeek'e k'et'on' beedoy yee yʉh nonługh yʉh tʉkkʉhedegheeghel. Dehoon nonaan yedaalkkaanh. Ts'ʉh yeetl-deyh.

It was swimming across. It looked as if the caribou would turn around if it saw him. K'etetaal-kkaanee got into his canoe and paddled up to it. What did they think they were doing following him? Many of them jumped into their leaf canoes and covered the water. K'etetaalkkaanee went up to the caribou and shot it with an arrow.

Yeneeghok'etaatlkaanh. Go k'edeeteey helonh soohoonaaneyh yʉh yetl'odetaałdok go dek'es-kkaah nee ts'en', go bedzeyh de-beedoy eyeetlkel yeł.

He began to pull it ashore. There were so many of them. He purposely began to bounce the canoe as he paddled, on the pretext of dragging to shore the caribou that he had tied to the canoe.

"Haa! Nʉgh betode ghʉ ede-ghoyeneeghaalʉhdeneek," ts'ed-nee dehoon nonługh zo yeggen nozeghel. Nʉ'unzelnenh hu yʉh go too denhebelee' gheelhee. Go k'edeeteey helonh. Hedeelghos.

"Hey! Watch out for his waves," they said as they began to capsize. They were tipping over and drowning. There were a lot of them. They were all yelling.

Kk'ʉdaa no'o hʉkkʉyeelgges. Kk'ʉdaa ło'ts'eyʉh do'ooghe yʉh hebaahaa yʉh neheghedenoh, go helonh ts'en'. Go sołt'aanh gheel hʉn, "Seyots'aa' k'ek'uh kk'aa dedeyoh." Nedaanh k'edee bedenaa' taałdlee'? "Seyots'aa' k'ek'ʉh kk'aa dedeyoh. Seyots'aa' k'ek'ʉh kk'aa dedeyoh. Nʉgh seyots'aa' k'ek'ʉh kk'aa dent'aa," neey yʉh do'o yʉh dotaalnee'.

He pulled the caribou ashore. The place seemed to be alive with little people on the shore as he worked on it. A woman kept telling him, "My daughter has developed a taste for fat." Was her child starving or what? "My daugher has developed a taste for fat. My daughter has developed a taste for fat." He gave her some but she kept coming back for more, saying, "My daughter has developed a taste for fat."

K'enooł haayedeneeggodle aahaa yoonee'ʉh. Soohoonaay eeydee yʉh yekk'e dol'ʉh. No'o t'aanh soot'e naaghedenoh kk'e deghet'aa' de naagheteedenolaa.

He tore a piece of lacy membrane from the stomach and threw it at her.[2] He threw it over her on purpose. While he was working he saw that the membrane was moving around for a while. Then it stopped.

Dehoon kk'ʉdaa ło'ts'eyʉh kk'ʉdaa go nek'etaatl-'ʉhtl. "Go ło eeydenh hodee? Go ło eeydenh hodee?" hedetaalnee'. Go k'enooł gheel heetaatlkoodee. Nedaats'e haahaa ghulaa' heyekk'aa eelneek.

He continued to butcher the caribou. Soon they began to say, "Where is she? Where is she?" They began to pick up the fat. I guess that is how they found out what he had done.

"Haa! Dont'aa go k'enooł-yekk'e doltlaakk k'ek'uh yekk'e doltlaakk. Nʉgh ees soohooneey ent'aa nʉgh deyeeloh," hedetaalnee'. "Lʉhłghaa." Go koon bedzeyh doots'aa koon ehendeneyh.

"Hey! He threw the membrane over her. He threw the fat on top of her. He did it on purpose," they started to say. "Kill him." I don't know how they expected to do that when they could not even kill a

2. *K'enooł* is the omentum, a fatty membrane that surrounds the stomach and looks somewhat like lace. The woman who had been bothering him was a camp robber woman.

"Nʉgh lʉhłghaa. Nʉgh sołt'aanh bʉgh hootsenenh aahaa k'edegge dedeyoh. Lʉhłghaa!" koon kk'ʉdaa yʉh yee dohʉdegheelet. Hʉyee dohʉdegheelet.

caribou. "Kill him. He killed a very precious woman. Kill him!" they clamored. It was noisy.

Ts'ʉh taadleghel soohoonaaney.

He pretended to run away.

Kk'ʉdaa tl'ogho yʉh k'enodzen kk'o' aahaa yʉh k'uh kk'e deheye-taaldleen' gheelhee go daaheyedee-taatldek ts'en'. Ts'ʉh yoonł hok'ede-taałt'ekk. Eet etltaanh. Eet etltaanh.

They shot little arrows at him, and it was as if he were being cov-ered with quills. He threw himself forward and lay on the ground, pretending to be dead. He lay there.

Huyeł, "Dʉhłkk'oyh! Dʉhł-kk'oyh!" beeznee. Go hʉyts'en' ts'ʉh kk'ʉdaa kk'aa nohʉnaalyonh. K'etsaan' kuh yʉh tʉgh hedetaal-tlaatl. K'etsaan' tʉgh hedetlaał. Ts'ʉh eeydee yʉh heyetleeghodaal-tonh. K'etsaan' heyetleeghodaal-tonh. Ts'ʉh kk'ʉdaa heyaakkun'-daaneełtleyh. Yoogh bʉkkʉndaa-dletluh.

"Burn him! Burn him!" they said. It was fall and the grass was mature. They chopped down grass and piled it on top of him. Then they lit the grass but it burned on top without harming him.

Ts'ʉh eet etltaa---nh. Heye-deełkk'onh. Go daaheyoolaah? Go k'edeeteey nekoh.

He lay there as if he were dead. They had burned him. They could not do anything else with him, he was so big.

Kk'ʉdaa hʉn hʉdeedetl'eets go kk'ʉdaa hʉyts'en'. Ts'e gheel go bedzeyh kk'o'eededaalee. Kk'ʉdaa hʉdeedetl'eets dehoon degge daa-noneełneek. Ts'ʉh daa'en taalyo.

Soon it was dark, being early in the fall. That was why the caribou had been on the move. It was dark and they had all gone, so he got up. He began to walk. A

Huyeł nedaa dodʉggʉ hʉn negoodzegh donaaldo. Ts'ʉh noyegheek'enh. Naa'en neenoyeeltaanh.

Dehoon go bedzeyh gheel łaaheltaayee.

Kk'ʉdaa eeydee ghenee hʉdeełkk'onh. Ts'ʉh eeydee ekkʉneek'egheełtleyh. Go yetlee' koonh.

Huyeł hʉn, "Dont'aa no'o nogheedeno'! No'o ees hʉdeełkk'onh! No'o ees nogheedeno'!" beeznee.

Huyeł hʉn kk'ʉdaa, "K'etohhon' de onee'. K'etohhon' detlekts'e onee'," hʉdetaalnee'. Ts'ʉh go too aahaa koon k'ʉhʉdeeghʉnh. Ts'ʉh kk'ʉdaa heyʉghʉ neeneedaatl, k'eldon' kkaa yaan'. Kk'ʉdaa no'ots'e denaa een k'etohon heyʉgh needenaadeggut. Ts'ʉh neełk'ots'en kkun' ghʉ neehedenaadeggut. Dehoon nonł kk'ʉdaa k'etaalt'aa'. Nonł k'et'aał. K'etlee' ekkʉneek'eghee'o.

K'enoggaadze dledʉh. Yaats'en kkʉnok'elt'aa'. Yaats'enyee koon dledʉh. At'eeyło koon detoneeł yełnee dehʉgh go yetlee' ekkʉneek'egheełtleyh. Yaats'en koon kkʉnok'elt'aa'. Huyeł no'o daadletl'een kkaa hʉn, "Nʉgh lʉhłghaa," heyenodetaałnee'.

great horned owl landed on a tree near him and he shot it down with an arrow and took it back to the village.

The little people were feasting on the caribou.

He built a fire to cook the owl. He put it on a roasting stick, including the head.

"He's alive over there! He built a fire! He's alive over there!" they said.

K'etetaalkkaanee said, "Come eat. Everybody come eat," he told them. This was after he had drowned so many of them. Some of them gathered around him. The people who wanted to eat came to him. Some sat on one side of the fire, and some on the other. The owl was beginning to cook with its head on the cooking stick.

Soon one of the eyes popped out and everybody on one side of the campfire died from its steam. Then the other eye popped out. Evidently he had meant for that to happen. That is why he put the head on a stick as well. Everybody on the other side of the fire died too. The few left began to yell, "Kill him!"

Ts'ʉh go debeedoy debeedoy tonogheetonh. Taadleghel soohoonaaney. Kk'ʉdaa neek'oneekkaanh. Nonł noneets'e yʉh saakkaay yeł detlekts'e gheelhee nedaats'e ghulaa'.

He put his canoe back into the water and pretended to flee. They all followed him in their canoes, all the children and everybody.

Bekk'e koon kk'ʉdaa tl'ogho yʉh tokkokk'e yʉh haahoodeet'aanaa ts'e denohoodeyoh. Dehoon kk'ʉdaa tl'ogho yʉh yetl'odetaałedok. Tl'ogho yʉh todeteteeyh!

The water was black behind him, there were so many of them. Then he began to make waves by bouncing up and down in his canoe. There were big waves!

"Nʉgh betode'," hednee. Neełts'e hedelghus. Dehoon no'oogh zo yʉh yeggennaahedelnenh. Yeggennaahedelnenh. Detlekts'e hebekkele.

"Watch out for his waves," they said. They shouted to each other. They were capsizing all around him. Soon they were all gone.

Ts'ʉh go bʉgh neek'ots'eneedaatlne detlege koon ʉhʉdeeghʉnh. Kk'ʉdaa k'eełekk'enh zokk'ʉł k'edo'eełtaalaa.

Then he killed the remaining ones on shore. He did not even save one person.

Et'eeyło k'oyeedenaa kkaa. K'oyeedenaa. Go nedaats'e ghulaa' go k'oyeedenaa? Kk'edonts'ednee kkenaage'. Et'eeyło k'oyeedenaa kkaa koon kk'ʉdaa hʉdeeghʉnh. Yʉhʉ go doogh hebehootołdlaa'aa dʉhʉgh gheelhee degheenee' koon, go Grandpa gheelaa'.

Apparently they were little people. Little people. I don't understand the word *k'oyeedenaa,* which is used to refer to the little people. It is old language from the Distant Time stories. He had killed all the little people. My grandpa said that he had done this so that they would not be around today.

Yełkuh Sołt'aanh
Giant Woman

Ts'ʉh kk'ʉdaa yoogh kk'ʉdaa hʉyts'en'. Nodo' needze ghekkaał. Ghekkaał. Ehuyeł gheel go kk'ʉdaa yoodo hʉn koon kk'ʉdaa hʉdaal-kk'un'. Ts'ʉh kk'ʉdaa eet neegho-neekkaanh. Doogh tolyo. Huyeł hʉn go hʉn sołt'aanh ku---h. Et'eeyło yełkuh sołt'aanh hʉn ledo.

Doogh debaats'e k'aal ghodo-k'eghedeetaałno' gheelhee. Yeyeł tsondodetaałdlee'.

Huyeł gheel go, "Haa! Hʉ-deeyh! Hʉdok'edee netsey ten he'eenlenh ts'e koon dent'aanh," yełnee. "Tlaa eey dent'aanh ts'e hogho aay'oo doghʉn hʉneede-ghee'oy deneentlelaaa'," yełnee. No'o ts'ebaa laał ts'ebaa kuh aay'oo hʉneedeghee'o. Ts'ʉh eeydee ghʉ neeneeyo. Ts'ʉh kk'ʉdaa yedenaal-tleł. Go tlaa eey donaahoogholtsoł soo'u haahaa yełnee ts'en'.

Ts'ʉh kk'ʉdaa no'ots'e yʉgh neeno'eedeyo. Kk'ʉdaa debaats'e k'aal yeł naaltaanh. Huyeł betsoo konh toyegheełtlaakk, go k'edee-teey negudze. Lekkon yaan' nelaanh ts'e honotoyegheełtlaakk.

It was almost fall. He paddled along downstream. Once again, he went around a bend and saw a camp farther downriver. He paddled to it, landed, and walked up the bank. A very big woman was there. Evidently she was a giant.

He began to tease the old lady and flirt with her.

"Hey! Watch it! Are you sure that you're big enough to follow your grandpa's path?" she asked him. "If you're really so strong, why don't you cut down that tree on the hillside?" she told him. A big spruce tree stood on the hillside. He went to it and he chopped it down. That had been her way of testing his strength.

Then he went back to her house and lay down beside her. He got washed into the old lady's stomach, he was so little. He floated out, covered with blood, and flew away as a pine

Huyeł kaayoode nelaanh ts'e ee-t'ʉkk. Beeznee de hʉyaan' hʉkk'e beyeł eseneyh.

Et'eghł hʉydo hʉtaaldlet yeenslenh. Hʉyh ghon' naaltlgus.

grosbeak.[1] That is as far as I know the story.

I thought the winter had just begun. I've chewed off part of it.

1. That is why the pine grosbeak has a rosy red breast and head. The pine grosbeak is also called *kk'ogholdaale* "the traveler" and *dʉkkʉghʉldaal* "that which eats seeds on tree branches or treetops."